Windows Phone 7.5 Data Cookbook

Over 30 recipes for storing, managing, and manipulating data in Windows Phone 7.5 Mango applications

Ramesh Thalli

PUBLISHING

BIRMINGHAM - MUMBAI

Windows Phone 7.5 Data Cookbook

First published: October 2011

Production Reference: 1181011

Published by Packt Publishing Ltd.
Livery Place
35 Livery Street
Birmingham B3 2PB, UK.

ISBN 978-1-84969-122-2

www.packtpub.com

Cover Image by Asher Wishkerman (a.wishkerman@mpic.de)

Credits

Author
Ramesh Thalli

Reviewers
John Baird

Feyaerts David

Atley Hunter

Ian T. Lackey

Acquisition Editor
Steven Wilding

Development Editors
Gaurav Mehta

Hithesh Uchil

Technical Editor
Llewellyn F. Rozario

Copy Editor
Neha Shetty

Project Coordinator
Kushal Bhardwaj

Proofreader
Chris Smith

Indexer
Hemangini Bari

Production Coordinator
Arvindkumar Gupta

Cover Work
Arvindkumar Gupta

About the Author

Ramesh Thalli is a Senior Application Architect and a developer who has over 15 years of experience in the Microsoft Windows development environment. He has worked extensively in WinForms, ASP.NET, WPF, Silverlight, SQL Server and is proficient in C, C++, and C# languages. He has conducted many live and online training workshops in Microsoft technologies. He has a passion for Mobile Operating Systems, which includes iPhone, Android, and WP7.

He specializes in building enterprise applications in IT Support Functions such as Project Portfolio Management, Project Management, HR Systems, IT Governance, Enterprise Architecture, IT Finance, and Software Estimation.

He has extensive experience in the telecom and healthcare insurance industries. In his spare time, he loves to teach and also has a keen interest in exploring world percussion instruments.

First, I would like to thank everyone at Packt Publishing for making this book a reality. Secondly, I would like to thank my wife, Roopa, for believing in me and helping me complete this book successfully. Last, but not the least, I would like to thank my family and friends, in particular Sujeeth Narayan, Gordon Durich, and Shravan Tedla for giving their feedback and encouraging me.

About the Reviewers

John Baird is the founder of XamlWare, a professional consulting firm specializing in Silverlight and Windows Phone 7 development. John has 30 years of experience designing, coding, and implementing software solutions.

John co-founded the Northern Delaware .Net Users group. He is heavily involved in the local .Net communities, and travels extensively giving presentations to user groups, code camps, and special-interest groups.

John is also a four-time recipient of Microsoft's MVP award and is a part of the exclusive group of 23 MVPs chosen to be a Windows Phone 7 MVP.

Feyaerts David has worked on .Net technologies for more than three years. After having completed a Bachelor's degree in Informatique and System, he worked as a software engineer at Bizzdev (Belgium).

He especially works on C# and .Net (mobile and desktop applications), and was quickly promoted to a project leader. He works on multiple projects such as desktop application, mobile application (Windows Mobile and Windows Phone), ASP website, and so on.

To validate his expertise on .Net technologies, he is both a Microsoft Certified Professional Developer (MCPD) and Microsoft Certified Technology Specialist (MCTS) on Silverlight 4.

As a mobile developer for his employer he participates in development of an e-Health application for Windows Phone 7. He appreciates the WP7 platform since it is easy to use and provides new opportunities of design.

During personal time, he also works independently as a developer for Windows Phone applications. At the time of writing, he is working on his fourth application.

Atley Hunter has been a professional developer for over 15 years and was a mobile developer way before it was cool. Atley is constantly pushing devices to do more. As an MVP in Windows Phone Development with over 40 apps under his belt and numerous talks, blog postings, and HackFests, he is continually working to expand his development knowledge and share it with anyone who wants to learn.

When not at the computer or working with other developers, Atley is an avid adventurer and can be found snowboarding, rappelling, bungee jumping, skydiving, base jumping, mountain/rock/structure climbing or kayaking.

Active on LinkedIn (`http://www.linkedin.com/in/AtleyHunter`), Twitter (`http://twitter.com/AtleyHunter`), and on his blog (`www.atleyhunter.com`), Atley is never far from reach and is always happy to help.

Ian T. Lackey worked as a systems engineer for a St. Louis-based ISP from 1999 to 2002. At that time, he began developing web applications using ASP and migrated to ASP.NET shortly before the 2.0 release. Ian now works as a full-time programmer analyst II for the Pediatrics department of Washington University's School of Medicine. He also runs a small business, DigitalSnap Inc. (`http://www.digitalsnap.net`) that provides custom Silverlight software, individual DotNetNuke modules (`http://www.itlackey.net`), as well as custom and commercial Windows Phone 7 applications.

Currently Ian is involved in community-driven areas such as the OpenLight Group (`http://www.openlightgroup.net`), which manages open source projects including several DotNetNuke modules and many Silverlight-based applications. He is also a registered iNeta speaker and is involved with the St. Louis .NET user group (`http://www.ineta.org`). Ian currently lives in a small town in Illinois, just East of St. Louis, with his wife Julie (`http://www.calljulie.info`) and two daughters, Britney and Brooklyn.

> To everyone in my life, I truly thank you all for the love and support you have so graciously provided throughout the years!

www.PacktPub.com

Support files, eBooks, discount offers and more

You might want to visit www.PacktPub.com for support files and downloads related to your book.

Did you know that Packt offers eBook versions of every book published, with PDF and ePub files available? You can upgrade to the eBook version at www.PacktPub.com and as a print book customer, you are entitled to a discount on the eBook copy. Get in touch with us at service@packtpub.com for more details.

At www.PacktPub.com, you can also read a collection of free technical articles, sign up for a range of free newsletters and receive exclusive discounts and offers on Packt books and eBooks.

http://PacktLib.PacktPub.com

Do you need instant solutions to your IT questions? PacktLib is Packt's online digital book library. Here, you can access, read and search across Packt's entire library of books.

Why Subscribe?

- Fully searchable across every book published by Packt
- Copy and paste, print and bookmark content
- On demand and accessible via web browser

Free Access for Packt account holders

If you have an account with Packt at www.PacktPub.com, you can use this to access PacktLib today and view nine entirely free books. Simply use your login credentials for immediate access.

I like to dedicate this book to my sons, Surya and Pranav, who represent the future gadget generation to whom I would like to pass on the Windows experience.

Table of Contents

Preface

Storing and manipulating data plays an important role in making any mobile phone effective in business applications or any other data-driven application. *Windows Phone 7.5 Data Cookbook* covers topics such as how to bind data easily using databinding techniques, how to save data in local storage for later retrieval, how to format XML for data storage, exploring on-device databases for storage options, how to consume cloud data sources like OData, REST, and WCF, and finally, how to scale applications using the most popular MVVM pattern.

This book has a wide range of simple to complex recipes, which help you understand basic concepts of data handling. You will be able to apply the knowledge you gained from these recipes to build your own apps effectively. Instead of diving into writing complex sample applications for the first time, this book focuses on simplifying the concepts in an easy step-by-step fashion using simple straightforward samples.

Windows Phone 7.5 Data Cookbook will make you an expert in the areas of data access and storage. When you are ready to start developing a data-driven Windows Phone 7 application, you will be well equipped with the different scenarios to implement and store data.

What this book covers

Chapter 1, Databinding to UI Elements, shows how to create data binding to User Interface elements using any data sources such as CLR Objects, files, XML, or external databases. Various topics such as Element Binding, DataContext, DataTemplates, DataMode, and Data Converters are covered. Finally, a simple app is created applying the different databinding concepts.

Chapter 2, Isolated Storage, demonstrates how to open, create, and save user settings to local isolated storage for later consumption, using name/value pairs or images or XML files.

Chapter 3, XML as a Data Store, covers how to open a local or remote XML file, how to navigate the XML file to search for specific information, and finally, how to serialize XML to an object.

Chapter 4, Using Open Data, explains how to consume OData with a simple URI and then how to search with different operations. Finally, it demonstrates how to execute CRUD operations with OData.

Chapter 5, Using On-device Databases, explores different on-device database options available such as commercial Perst, open source SQLite, and Microsoft's SQL CE. It also explains how to use LINQ to SQL in SQL CE.

Chapter 6, Representational State Transfer—REST, covers basic concepts of consuming REST services and calling different social media services such as Twitter and RSS Feeds. Finally, it demonstrates how to build a simple REST service.

Chapter 7, Windows Communication Foundation–WCF, demonstrates how to create and consume simple web services and understand LINQ features. It demonstrates how to build services using ADO.NET Entity Data Model and LINQ to SQL. Both these technologies significantly automate building service layers quickly and effectively.

Chapter 8, Model View ViewModel, introduces us to basic concepts of the MVVM design pattern and how it can be implemented using simple samples. MVVM Light toolkit is introduced by demonstrating different scenarios of applications. Finally, a sample is created to demonstrate how easy it will be to maintain a MVVM-patterned application.

What you need for this book

The following is the list of software needed for this book. Different software and tools are used during the course of this book to demonstrate specific concepts or techniques.

1. Microsoft Visual Studio 2010 Express for Windows Phone
   http://www.microsoft.com/visualstudio/en-us/products/2010-editions/windows-phone-developer-tools

2. Microsoft Visual Studio Web Developer 2010 Express
   http://www.microsoft.com/visualstudio/en-us/products/2010-editions/visual-web-developer-express

3. SQL Server 2008 Manager Express
   http://www.microsoft.com/download/en/details.aspx?id=26729

4. SQL CE Edition 4.0
   http://go.microsoft.com/fwlink/?LinkId=212219

5. SQLite Studio
   http://sqlitestudio.one.pl/

6. SQLite Client
   http://sqlitewindowsphone.codeplex.com/releases

7. Microsoft Web Matrix
   http://www.asp.net/web-pages

8. Perst.Net
   `http://www.mcobject.com`

9. MVVMLight toolkit
   `http://mvvmlight.codeplex.com/`

10. Phone 7 toolkit
    `http://silverlight.codeplex.com/releases`

Who this book is for

This book is for developers who understand the language features of C#, XAML, and Silverlight technologies, and want to build data-driven apps, or line-of-business (LOB) applications using Windows Mobile platform. It helps if the developer has some understanding of Metro design philosophy and user interface guidelines from Microsoft. Also, this book helps developers of other mobile platforms to convert their apps to Windows Phone 7.

Conventions

In this book, you will find a number of styles of text that distinguish between different kinds of information. Here are some examples of these styles, and an explanation of their meaning.

Code words in text are shown as follows: "First, create a private variable for `DataClass` before the `MainPage` constructor."

A block of code is set as follows:

```
namespace Recipe2
{
  public class DataClass
  {
    public string Name { get; set; }
    public string Notes { get; set; }
  }
}
```

When we wish to draw your attention to a particular part of a code block, the relevant lines or items are set in bold:

```
<TextBlock x:Name="ApplicationTitle" Text="Phone7 Recipes"
  Style="{StaticResource PhoneTextNormalStyle}"/>
```

Any command-line input or output is written as follows:

```
datasvcutil /uri:http://services.odata.org/
  (S(bltvbobialrthiavqczdcrlu))/OData/OData.svc/ /out:.
  \EditODataModel.cs /Version:2.0 /DataServiceCollection
```

New terms and **important words** are shown in bold. Words that you see on the screen, in menus or dialog boxes for example, appear in the text like this: "Click on the **New Query** icon in the tab bar and then **Execute** the selected query."

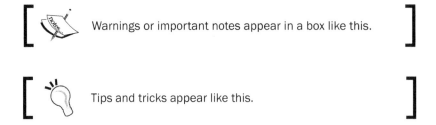

Warnings or important notes appear in a box like this.

Tips and tricks appear like this.

Reader feedback

Feedback from our readers is always welcome. Let us know what you think about this book— what you liked or may have disliked. Reader feedback is important for us to develop titles that you really get the most out of.

To send us general feedback, simply send an e-mail to feedback@packtpub.com, and mention the book title via the subject of your message.

If there is a book that you need and would like to see us publish, please send us a note in the **SUGGEST A TITLE** form on www.packtpub.com or e-mail suggest@packtpub.com.

If there is a topic that you have expertise in and you are interested in either writing or contributing to a book, see our author guide on www.packtpub.com/authors.

Customer support

Now that you are the proud owner of a Packt book, we have a number of things to help you to get the most from your purchase.

Downloading the example code

You can download the example code files for all Packt books you have purchased from your account at http://www.PacktPub.com. If you purchased this book elsewhere, you can visit http://www.PacktPub.com/support and register to have the files e-mailed directly to you.

Errata

Although we have taken every care to ensure the accuracy of our content, mistakes do happen. If you find a mistake in one of our books—maybe a mistake in the text or the code—we would be grateful if you would report this to us. By doing so, you can save other readers from frustration and help us improve subsequent versions of this book. If you find any errata, please report them by visiting http://www.packtpub.com/support, selecting your book, clicking on the **errata submission form** link, and entering the details of your errata. Once your errata are verified, your submission will be accepted and the errata will be uploaded on our website, or added to any list of existing errata, under the Errata section of that title. Any existing errata can be viewed by selecting your title from http://www.packtpub.com/support.

Piracy

Piracy of copyright material on the Internet is an ongoing problem across all media. At Packt, we take the protection of our copyright and licenses very seriously. If you come across any illegal copies of our works, in any form, on the Internet, please provide us with the location address or website name immediately so that we can pursue a remedy.

Please contact us at copyright@packtpub.com with a link to the suspected pirated material. We appreciate your help in protecting our authors, and our ability to bring you valuable content.

Questions

You can contact us at questions@packtpub.com if you are having a problem with any aspect of the book, and we will do our best to address it.

1
Data Binding to UI Elements

In this chapter, we will cover:

- ▶ Element Binding
- ▶ DataContext
- ▶ DataTemplates
- ▶ How DataMode is used
- ▶ Converting data for display
- ▶ Building a Simple App

Introduction

Data binding in Windows Phone 7 is basically connecting the UI Element with any data source. The data source may be a CLR Object, File, XML, RSS/Atom, SQL Server Database, ODATA, or any web service. The data source can reside on either on-device or external sources. Data binding is a powerful feature that makes it easy to tie UI elements to data elements in one simple property.

In this chapter, we will look into different aspects of data binding. In the first recipe we will learn how to declare **Binding** properties for a textbox element. Then, you will be introduced to **DataContext**, which is very important for connecting the data to UI elements. **DataContext** is also very important for separating the **View** from the **Model**, which is used in the **MVVM** (**Model-View-ViewModel**) pattern. We will learn how **DataTemplates** make it easy to reuse templates. **DataMode** helps in setting the Databinding to one way or two way updates. **Notification** sends the refresh notification to UI elements that data has been updated. Finally, we will learn about **Converters** and how they can be used to convert and format the displayed data.

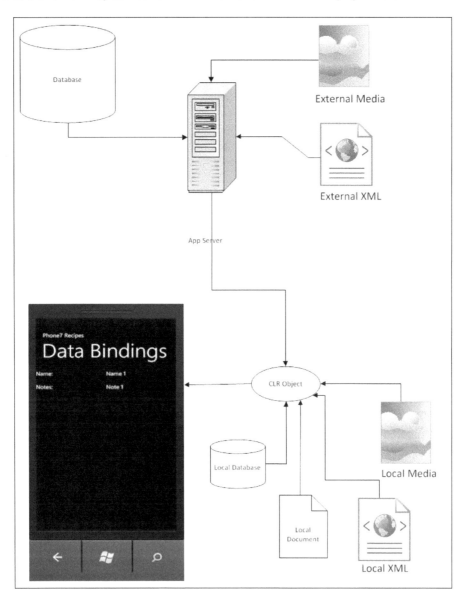

Element binding

In our first recipe, let's learn how to create XAML elements and about data binding to another control like textbox using the ElementName property of the binding object.

Getting ready

1. Open the Visual Studio for Phone 7 and create a Windows Phone Application. Name the application Recipe1 and click on **OK**.

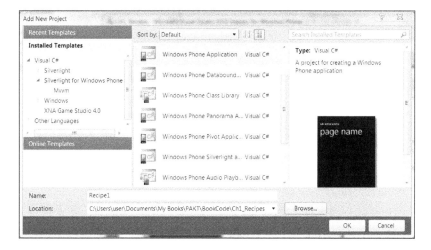

2. A shell application with default files is added as shown in the following screenshot. Notice that there are several files added to the project by default. The App.xaml file contains the App constructor with different App event handlers included in the App.xaml.cs file. There are three image files; ApplicationIcon.png is for the App Icon displayed in the Phone, Background.png is the default background image of the app, and SplashScreenImage.jpg can be used for flashing the screen before the app launches. MainPage.xaml is the main page to be displayed when the app is launched. This is where we add all the display elements for the application. The MainPage.xaml.cs file is where all the code is added to manipulate the data.

3. After you open the project, just press *F5* and run it to make sure there are no errors. It is good practice to run the app as often as you can so you can resolve any issue, otherwise you end up accumulating too many bugs.

How to do it...

Let's build a simple display page where we have one textbox to enter data and a text block to display it. When you enter text in the textbox you will see it is displayed in the display text block.

1. Let's change the application title and the page title text blocks in the `MainPage.xaml.cs` file. Open the file and look for `StackPanel` with `Name TitlePanel`.

```
<!--TitlePanel contains the name of the application and page
  title-->

<StackPanel x:Name="TitlePanel" Grid.Row="0"
  Grid.ColumnSpan ="2">>
  <TextBlock x:Name="ApplicationTitle" Text="Ch1 Recipes"
    Style="{StaticResource PhoneTextNormalStyle}"/>
  <TextBlock x:Name="PageTitle" Text="Element Name"
    Style="{StaticResource PhoneTextTitle1Style}"/>
</StackPanel>
```

Downloading the example code

You can download the example code files for all Packt books you have purchased from your account at `http://www.PacktPub.com`. If you purchased this book elsewhere, you can visit `http://www.PacktPub.com/support` and register to have the files e-mailed directly to you.

2. In order to display two columns and three rows, we should change the Grid `ColumnDefinition` and `RowDefinition` as illustrated in the XAML snippet. Locate this inside the `Grid` named `LayoutRoot`:

```
<Grid.RowDefinitions>
  <RowDefinition Height="Auto"/>
  <RowDefinition Height="81"/>
  <RowDefinition Height="526*"/>
</Grid.RowDefinitions>

<Grid.ColumnDefinitions>
  <ColumnDefinition Width="159*"></ColumnDefinition>
  <ColumnDefinition Width="321*"></ColumnDefinition>
</Grid.ColumnDefinitions>
```

3. Add three `TextBlock` elements and a text element inside the `ContentPanel` grid. Here we will add binding information to the `tbNameDisplayContent` control. `ElementName` is assigned to `TextBox` control name. `Path` is assigned to the `Text` property of the `TextBox` control; this is where the data is fetched.

```
<Grid x:Name="ContentPanel" Grid.Row="1" Grid.RowSpan="2"
  Grid.ColumnSpan="2" Margin="0,0,0,-16">

  <TextBlock x:Name ="tbName" Text ="Name:"
    Margin="2,13,371,582" />

  <TextBox x:Name ="txtNameContent" Text =""
    Margin="128,0,6,567" />

  <TextBlock x:Name ="tbNameDisplay" Text ="Display Name:"
    Height="43" VerticalAlignment="Top" Margin="2,94,0,0"
    HorizontalAlignment="Left" Width="133" />

  <TextBlock x:Name ="tbNameDisplayContent" Text ="{Binding
    ElementName=txtNameContent, Path=Text}"
    Margin="140,100,24,505" />

</Grid>
```

4. Press *F5*; now enter a name in the textbox and as you type you will see the text in the display text block, as shown in the following screenshot. This is the power of Data Binding.

How it works...

We used the `Binding` class in the `XAML` using the following shorthand syntax:

```
<object property="{Binding ElementName=name, Path=property}" …/>
```

You can either use `Path=Name` or just the name in the property `Path`. We set the binding information to the `Content` property of the `TextBlock` control. We used `ElementName` as the textbox control name and then we assigned the textbox control's `Text` property to the `Path`. Basically, the data source for the binding is the `Text` property of the textbox.

There's more...

In the last recipe, we learned how to use Binding with `ElementName` and `Path`. Similar to `Path`, we can use many properties like **Converter**, **Mode**, **StringFormat**, and so on. We will discuss the usage of these properties in the next several recipes in this chapter. For more information on Binding check this MSDN article:

```
http://msdn.microsoft.com/en-us/library/ms752347.aspx
```

See also

Check the recipes on *How DataMode is used* and *Converting data for display* in this chapter. Also, check the next recipe, which discusses the important concept of **DataContext**.

DataContext

In the last recipe, we discussed how the data binding is done at the element level. In this recipe, let's add some CLR Object and use the **DataContext** to link a Databound element and the property in the CLR Object.

Getting ready

Let's create a new project for this recipe. Right-click on the last solution folder **Ch1_Recipes** and **Add | New Project**, select the Windows Phone Application Template, and name it `Ch1_Recipe2`.

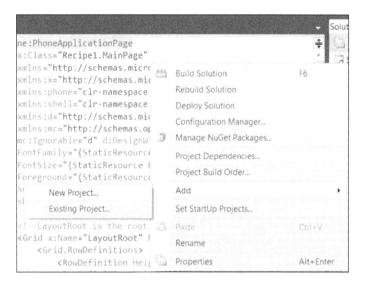

How to do it...

Here, let's create a simple application to tie data elements with a CLR Object. A data class with just two properties is created and then initialized to some test data. Then, it is assigned to the data context.

1. Right-click on **Ch1_Recipe2** and **Add | Class**.

2. Create the class, name it `DataClass` and add just two string properties; one called `Name` and the other `Notes`:

```
namespace Recipe2
{
  public class DataClass
  {
    public string Name { get; set; }
    public string Notes { get; set; }
  }
}
```

3. Open the `MainPage.xaml` file and change the `ApplicationTitle` and `PageTitle` as shown in the following code snippet:

```
<!--TitlePanel contains the name of the application and page
title-->

<StackPanel x:Name="TitlePanel" Grid.Row="0"
  Grid.ColumnSpan ="2">>
  <TextBlock x:Name="ApplicationTitle" Text="Phone7 Recipes"
    Style="{StaticResource PhoneTextNormalStyle}"/>
  <TextBlock x:Name="PageTitle" Text="Object Bindings"
    Style="{StaticResource PhoneTextTitle1Style}"/>
</StackPanel>
```

4. In order to display two columns and three rows, we should change the Grid `ColumnDefinition` and `RowDefinition` as illustrated in the following XAML snippet:

```
<!--LayoutRoot is the root grid where all page content is
  placed-->
<Grid x:Name="LayoutRoot" Background="Transparent">
  <Grid.RowDefinitions>
    <RowDefinition Height="Auto"/>
    <RowDefinition Height="50"/>
    <RowDefinition Height="*"/>
  </Grid.RowDefinitions>

  <Grid.ColumnDefinitions>
    <ColumnDefinition Width="74*"></ColumnDefinition>
    <ColumnDefinition Width="406*"></ColumnDefinition>
  </Grid.ColumnDefinitions>
```

5. Let's add two `TextBlock` controls to display `Name` and `Notes`. Here the `Name` and `Notes` are referring to the properties of the Object `DataClass`. Add four `TextBlock` elements inside the `ContentPanel` grid; here we will add binding information to display both elements `tbNameContent` and `tbNoteContent`. Binding objects tie a name to a control object without knowing where it comes from, as follows:

```
<!--ContentPanel - place additional content here-->
<Grid x:Name="ContentPanel" Grid.Row="1" Grid.RowSpan="2"
  Grid.ColumnSpan="2" Margin="0,0,0,-16">

  <TextBlock x:Name ="tbName" Text ="Name:" Grid.Row="1"
    Grid.Column ="0"/>

  <TextBlock x:Name ="tbNameContent" Text ="{Binding Name}"
    Margin="74,0,6,567" />
```

```
    <TextBlock x:Name ="tbNotes" Text ="Notes:" Height="43"
      VerticalAlignment="Top" Margin="0,85,412,0" />

    <TextBlock x:Name ="tbNotesContent" Text ="{Binding Notes}"
      Margin="74,85,0,16" />
</Grid>
```

6. Press *F5*. Now you will see the two display items without any data, as follows:

7. Open the `MainPage.xaml.cs` file. First, create a private variable for `DataClass` before the `MainPage` constructor. In the `MainPage` constructor, initialize the `DataClass` object with sample data using the object initializer as shown in the following code snippet. Finally, `myData` object is assigned to `DataContext`, which updates the text blocks with the data.

```
namespace Recipe2
{
  public partial class MainPage : PhoneApplicationPage
  {

    private DataClass myData;

    // Constructor
    public MainPage()
    {
```

```
          InitializeComponent();
          // Initialize data class
          myData = new DataClass()
          {
            Name = "Name 1",
            Notes = "Note 1"
          };

          // Set the DataContext of the grid to DataClass Object
          LayoutRoot.DataContext = myData;
        }
      }
    }
```

8. Press *F5*. Now test data, which is initialized in the code behind the file, is displayed.

How it works...

Initially, we set the Binding properties of the elements to `DataClass` property names. Here the binding enables us to set the property names without actually knowing how they will be assigned later. Magic happens through the `DataContext`. The `DataContext` of the elements allows inheriting the information about the data, used for data binding, from their parent elements. Hence, setting the `DataContext` of `Layoutroot` to the `DataClass` object automatically applied to the text block elements with its properties.

There's more...

For more understanding of the `DataContext` class, check this MSDN resource online:

```
http://msdn.microsoft.com/en-us/library/system.windows.
frameworkelement.datacontext.aspx
```

How to export the project as a template

We will learn how to use `Recipe2` as a template so you can easily reuse the project as a starter application for future projects. You can export any of the projects you are working on as a template for future use.

1. Open the previous project `Recipe2`.

2. Go to **File | Export Template**.

3. Select the default project template as the option, which is `Recipe1`.

4. Fill in the Template Name `Ch1_Recipe` and click on **Finish**. The template is saved to your project template folder. Now, all the files are copied as a part of the project template `Ch1_Recipe`.

See also

Check the first recipe *Element Binding* to learn more about bindings. Also, check the next recipe on *Data Templates*.

Data Templates

Data Templates are a very powerful feature in XAML. Data Templates can be reusable within element level or application level. In this recipe, let's use the Data Template in the listbox control.

Getting ready

Let's create a new project using the template `Ch1_Recipe` and rename it as `Ch1_Recipe3`.

How to do it...

1. In this recipe we will give priority to the ListBox control.

2. Open the `MainPage.xaml` file, locate the `Grid` with the name `ContentPanel` and add a `TextBlock` and a `ListBox` after the last text block control. The `ListBox` control will contain `ItemTemplate` in which `DataTemplate` is added.

```xml
<!-- List box priority -->
<TextBlock x:Name ="tbPriority" Text ="Priority:"
  Grid.Row="3" Grid.Column ="0" />

<ListBox x:Name ="lstPriority" Grid.Row="3" Grid.Column ="1">
  <ListBox.ItemTemplate>
    <DataTemplate>
      <Border Name="border" BorderBrush="Red"
        BorderThickness="1" Padding="5" Margin="5">

      <StackPanel>
        <TextBlock x:Name ="tbPriorityContent" Text
          ="{Binding}" />
      </StackPanel>
      </Border>
    </DataTemplate>
  </ListBox.ItemTemplate>
</ListBox>
```

3. Let's initialize the `Listbox` in the code behind the XAML file, `MainPage.xaml.cs`, using the `ItemsSource` property of the `ListBox`. `ItemSource` is a collection property. Add the following code inside the `MainPage` constructor before the initialization:

```csharp
lstPriority.ItemsSource = new string[] { "Low", "Medium",
  "High" };
```

4. Press *F5* to see how the `ListBox` is filled with `Low`, `Medium`, and `High` values. Also, notice how the `ListBox` behavior changes with the `Border` style.

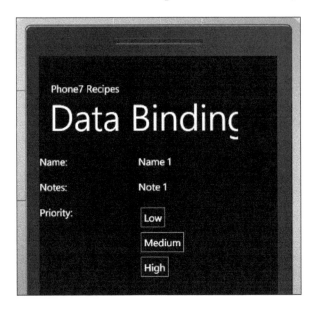

How it works...

A Data Template is the most flexible way to display data in XAML. It can include all the XAML controls like button, text blocks, textboxes, data grid, and so on. Here in the `ListBox` control, a Data Template is applied to all the items in the listbox along with all the formatting properties. We applied the `Red` border to the items in the `DataTemplate` mark-up.

There's more...

To understand more on Data Templates check the following article:

http://msdn.microsoft.com/en-us/library/ms742521.aspx

See also

Check the recipe named *DataContext* to understand more on data context concepts.

How DataMode is used

In this recipe let's understand the DataMode property of the Binding class. By default, the Data Mode property is **OneWay**. It has two other modes, **OneTime** and **TwoWay**. OneTime mode pulls the data only once from the source. OneWay mode only pulls the data from the source and updates it every time the source changes. TwoWay mode not only pulls the data from the source, but also pushes the changes back. These settings are not only used for data sources, they can also be tied to another element. Let's learn how we can use a TwoWay mode for the slider control to indicate the changes in a text block.

Getting ready

Create a new solution from the template Ch1_Recipe and name it Ch1_Recipe4_Mode.

How to do it...

1. Open the MainPage.xaml page and add a text block and a slider control to the existing page after the Notes text block. Here the slider control's value property is set to bind to text block control tbPriorityContent.

    ```
    <TextBlock x:Name ="tbPriorityContent" Text ="{Binding Priority}"
       Grid.Row="3" Grid.Column ="1" />


    <Slider x:Name ="slPriority" Width="300" Minimum="1"
       Maximum="10" Grid.Row="4" SmallChange="10" Grid.ColumnSpan ="2"
       Orientation="Horizontal" HorizontalAlignment="Left"
       Value="{Binding ElementName=tbPriorityContent, Path=Text,
       Mode=TwoWay}" />
    ```

2. Open the DataClass.cs file and add another property called Priority to the DataClass, as follows:

    ```
    public class DataClass
    {
      public string Name { get; set; }
      public string Notes { get; set; }
      public int Priority { get; set; }
    }
    ```

3. Open the MainPage.xaml.cs file and add another line in the object initializer to set the Priority to 8. This is illustrated in the following code:

    ```
    public MainPage()
    {
      InitializeComponent();
      // Initialize our data class
    ```

```
myData = new DataClass()
{
  Name = "Name 1",
  Notes = "Note 1",
  Priority = 8
};1

// Set the DataContext of the grid to DataClass
LayoutRoot.DataContext = myData;
```

4. Press *F5* to run the app. As we set the priority to 8, the slider will move automatically based on the text block `tbPriorityContent` content. Also, try to move the slider position and you will see the text block value also changing.

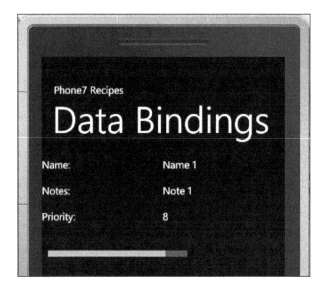

How it works...

You noticed that when the slider changes its position the priority text block gets updated automatically. Because of the two-way mode setting the text block gets the data updated in the control's property as soon as it is changed. Similarly, when the text block is initialized with a value, the slider value is changed. This demonstrates how the controls can be refreshed with two-way mode.

There's more...

To learn more on the Data Bindings topic check this MSDN article:

`http://msdn.microsoft.com/en-us/library/ms752347.aspx`

Check the recipes titled *Element Binding* and *DataContext* to learn more about these topics. Also, check the recipe *Building a Simple App*.

Converting data for display

On many occasions, we need to convert the data coming from the source into a form that is suitable for users to read. For example, we want to format a date as short date. In this recipe, let's add a date field to our CLR object and use the binding converter to display short date instead of long date.

Getting ready

For this recipe, let's copy the preceding project and name the new project as `Recipe5`. You can also do this by exporting the preceding project as a template and then creating the new project from this saved template.

How to do it...

1. Open the `DataClass.cs` file from the solution window. Add a new property `DateCreated`:

    ```
    public class DataClass
    {
      public string Name { get; set; }
      public string Notes { get; set; }
      public int Priority { get; set; }
      public DateTime DateCreated { get; set; }
    }
    ```

2. Add another class; as we are formatting the `Date` value, let's name it `DateFormatter`. In order for this class to inherit `IValueConverter`, you should use the `System.Windows.Data` namespace. Now add two functions `Convert` and `ConvertBack`:

    ```
    public class DateFormatter : IValueConverter
    {
      public object Convert(object value, Type targetType,
        object parameter, System.Globalization.CultureInfo culture)
      {
        string formatString = parameter as string;
        if (!string.IsNullOrEmpty(formatString))
        {
          return string. Format(culture, formatString, value);
        }
        return value.ToString();
    ```

```
    }
    public object ConvertBack(object value, Type targetType,
        object parameter, System.Globalization.CultureInfo culture)
    {
        throw new NotImplementedException();
    }
}
```

3. Open the `MainPage.xaml` and let's add the namespace at the top first as `PhoneApplicationPage` attribute.

```
xmlns:local="clr-namespace:Recipe5">
```

4. Now Add the `Resource` markup as shown in the following code snippet:

```
<phone:PhoneApplicationPage.Resources>
    <local:DateFormatter x:Key ="FormatConverter" />
</phone:PhoneApplicationPage.Resources>
```

5. Now, add two `TextBlock` controls for `DateCreated` column inside the `ListBox` control as shown in the following code snippet. Notice how the `Converter` property is set to a static resource with a converter parameter.

```
<TextBlock x:Name ="tbDateCreated" Text ="DateCreated:"
    Grid.Row="5" Grid.Column ="0" />
<TextBlock x:Name="tbDateCreatedContent" Grid.Row="5" Grid.Column
    ="1" Text="{Binding DateCreated,Converter={StaticResource
    FormatConverter}, ConverterParameter=\{0:d\}}" />
```

6. Add initialization data for the `DateCreated` field in the code behind the `XAML` file:

```
myData.DateCreated = DateTime.Now;
```

7. Press *F5* to run the code and you should see the following results:

How it works...

You can see that the `DateCreated` field is shorter than before. Converters are used for displaying the correct format of the data for users. In this recipe, `DateFormatter` uses string format to convert the date format. Similarly, various other conversions such as currency and percentage can be performed.

There's more...

You can learn deeper concepts related to data binding using this online resource:

`http://msdn.microsoft.com/en-us/library/ms752039.aspx`

See also

Check the recipes titled *DataContext* and *How DataMode is used* in this chapter.

Building a simple app

In this final recipe of this chapter, let's make use of all the knowledge we gained and apply it to one simple `MyTasks` App.

Getting ready

Right-click on the solution folder from the preceding recipe and navigate to **Open | New Project**. Select the Windows Phone 7 application project template. Name the project `Recipe5_MyTasks`.

How to do it...

Let's first build the UI for this app. This app will have two pages; the first page is the `main.xaml` file and the second one is the `add task.xaml` file.

1. Add an application bar at the bottom to provide navigation to the two pages that we are going to build in this app. The application bar is added, as shown in the following code snippet:

    ```
    <!--Sample code showing usage of ApplicationBar-->
    <phone:PhoneApplicationPage.ApplicationBar>
      <shell:ApplicationBar BackgroundColor="Orange" IsVisible="True"
        IsMenuEnabled="True">
        <shell:ApplicationBarIconButton
          IconUri="/Images/appbar.folder.rest.png"
          Click="ButtonFolder_Click" Text="Task Folder"/>
    ```

```
      <shell:ApplicationBarIconButton
        IconUri="/Images/appbar.add.rest.png"
        Click="ButtonAdd_Click" Text="Add Task"/>
    </shell:ApplicationBar>
  </phone:PhoneApplicationPage.ApplicationBar>
```

2. Right-click on the `Recipe5_MyTasks` project folder and add a new folder called `Images`.

3. Let's copy two images `appbar.folder.rest.png` and `appbar.add.rest.png` to this folder from `\Program Files (x86)\Microsoft SDKs\Windows Phone\ v7.1\Icons\light`. For a non-64 bit machine, you may navigate to `\Program Files\Microsoft SDKs\Windows Phone\v7.1\Icons\light`.

4. Right-click on the image files you added and select the **Build Action** property to **Content**. This will copy the images to an XAP file.

5. Open the `MainPage.xaml.cs` file and add two button event methods. The first button event, `ButtonFolder_Click`, uses the `NavigationService` class to navigate to `MainPage.xaml`. The second button event, `ButtonAdd_Click`, navigates to `AddTask.xaml` file:

```
private void ButtonFolder_Click(object sender, EventArgs e)
{
  NavigationService.Navigate(new Uri("/MainPage.xaml",
    UriKind.Relative));
}


private void ButtonAdd_Click(object sender, EventArgs e)
{
  NavigationService.Navigate(new Uri("/AddTask.xaml",
    UriKind.Relative));
}
```

6. Open the `Main.xaml` file and add the list box with its data template:

```
<!--ContentPanel - place additional content here-->
<Grid x:Name="ContentPanel" Margin="12,0,12,-13" Grid.Row="1">
  <ListBox x:Name ="lstTasks" Grid.Row="3" Grid.Column ="1">
    <ListBox.ItemTemplate>
      <DataTemplate>
        <Grid>
          <Grid.RowDefinitions>
            <RowDefinition/>
            <RowDefinition />
            <RowDefinition Height="15" />
          </Grid.RowDefinitions>

          <Grid.ColumnDefinitions>
```

```
          <ColumnDefinition Width="150" />
          <ColumnDefinition Width="200" />
          <ColumnDefinition Width="100" />
      </Grid.ColumnDefinitions>

      <TextBlock Grid.Row="0" Grid.Column="0" Text="{Binding
        Name}" />
      <TextBlock Grid.Row="0" Grid.Column="1" Text="{Binding
        DateDue}" />
      <TextBlock Grid.Row="0" Grid.Column="2" Text="{Binding
        Priority}" Forground = "{StaticResource
        PhoneAccentBrush}" />
      <TextBlock Grid.Row="1" Grid.ColumnSpan="3"
        Text="{Binding Notes}" />
      <TextBlock Grid.Row="2" Grid.ColumnSpan="3" />
    </Grid>
  </DataTemplate>
 </ListBox.ItemTemplate>
 </ListBox>
</Grid>
```

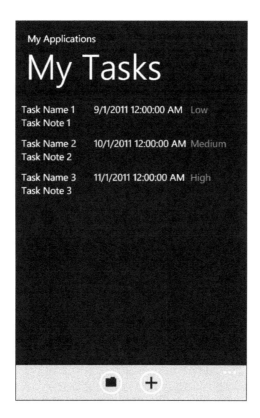

7. Open the `AddTask.xaml` file and add four text blocks in the `ContentPanel` grid:

```
<!--ContentPanel - place additional content here-->
<TextBlock x:Name="tbName" HorizontalAlignment="Left"
  TextWrapping="Wrap" Text="Name" VerticalAlignment="Top" />
<TextBlock x:Name="tbDescription" HorizontalAlignment="Left"
  Margin="8,70,0,0" TextWrapping="Wrap" Text="Description"
  VerticalAlignment="Top" />
<TextBlock x:Name="tbPriority" HorizontalAlignment="Left"
  Margin="8,150,0,0" TextWrapping="Wrap" Text="Priority"
  VerticalAlignment="Top" />
<TextBlock x:Name="tbDueDate" HorizontalAlignment="Left"
  Margin="8,277,0,0" TextWrapping="Wrap" Text="Due Date"
  VerticalAlignment="Top"/>
```

8. Now add corresponding textbox controls for each one, as follows:

```
<TextBox x:Name="txtName" Margin="119,0,70,0" TextWrapping="Wrap"
  VerticalAlignment="Top"/>
<TextBox x:Name="txtDescription" Margin="119,62,70,0"
  TextWrapping="Wrap" VerticalAlignment="Top"/>
<TextBox x:Name="txtDueDate" Margin="119,262,74,298"
  TextWrapping="Wrap"/>
<Button x:Name="btnAdd" Content="Add"  Margin="131,0,205,225"
  VerticalAlignment="Bottom" RenderTransformOrigin="0.969,0.514"
  Click="btnAdd_Click" />
<Button x:Name="btnCancel" Content="Cancel"
  HorizontalAlignment="Right"  Margin="0,0,74,225"
  VerticalAlignment="Bottom" Click="btnCancel_Click" />
<ListBox x:Name="lsyPriority" Margin="131,154,84,0"
  VerticalAlignment="Top">
  <ListBoxItem Content="Low"/>
  <ListBoxItem Content="Medium"/>
  <ListBoxItem Content="High"/>
</ListBox>
</Grid>
```

9. Right-click on the project folder and add a new class file. Name it `DataClass.cs`. Now, add the following `DataClass` with all its properties. If you compare this class with the preceding recipes, for simplicity we changed `int Priority` to `string Priority` and added one more `DateTime` property called `DateDue`.

```
public class DataClass
{
  public string Name { get; set; }
  public string Notes { get; set; }
  public string Priority { get; set; }
  public DateTime DateDue { get; set; }
  public DateTime DateCreated { get; set; }
}
```

10. Open the `MainPage.xaml.cs` file and add the `using` statement for the reference `System.Collections.ObjectModel`.

```
using System.Collections.ObjectModel;
```

11. `ObeservableCollection` is the collection class that we will use for building our task collection. Observable Collection provides the notifications whenever items get added or removed. Add the following line of code before the `MainPage` constructor method in the `MainPage.xaml.cs` file:

```
private ObservableCollection<DataClass> myTasks;
```

12. Let's add a method to initialize `myTasks`:

```
private void InitalizeTasks()
{
  myTasks = new ObservableCollection<DataClass>();
  DataClass myTask1 = new DataClass()
  {
    Name = "Task Name 1",
    Notes = "Task Note 1",
    Priority = "Low",
    DateDue = new DateTime(2011, 9, 1),
    DateCreated = DateTime.Now
  };
  myTasks.Add(myTask1);

  DataClass myTask2 = new DataClass()
  {
    Name = "Task Name 2",
    Notes = "Task Note 2",
    Priority = "Medium",
    DateDue = new DateTime(2011, 10, 1),
    DateCreated = DateTime.Now
  };
  myTasks.Add(myTask2);

  DataClass myTask3 = new DataClass()
  {
    Name = "Task Name 3",
    Notes = "Task Note 3",
    Priority = "High",
    DateDue = new DateTime(2011, 11, 1),
    DateCreated = DateTime.Now
  };
  myTasks.Add(myTask3);
}
```

13. Initialize this in the `MainPage` constructor and assign the `myTasks` collection to the listbox `itemsource` property:

```
public MainPage()
{
  InitializeComponent();
  InitalizeTasks();
  lstTasks.ItemsSource = myTasks;
}
```

14. Press *F5* and check out the results.

How it works...

In this recipe we created a display of the list of tasks in the `ListBox` and a form to add a new task to the list.

We initialized the tasks using the `ObeservableCollection` class and then added static data to this collection using the `Add` method.

Once the collection was built, we bound this list to `ListBox` for display. We added a navigation bar using the built-in `ApplicationBar` and then added two icons, one for adding a task to the list and another for navigating back to the main page.

There's more...

In the previous recipe, we mainly covered how to create the data binding for the main page list and then navigate to a new form to add the task. We can also add another important feature to select a list item and then update the existing data.

See also

Check the recipes in *Chapter 2*, *Isolated Storage*, to learn how to save the tasks to local storage. Also, check *Chapter 3*, *XML as a Data Store*, to learn how to save the tasks to XML files.

2
Isolated Storage

In this chapter, we will cover:

- ▸ Saving user settings
- ▸ Opening a file
- ▸ Creating a file
- ▸ Saving username and password
- ▸ Saving an image

Introduction

In Windows Phone 7 environment, local storage is the space available for each application. We can read and write data in this area, but we do not have access to other applications' storage areas or direct access file systems. **Isolated storage** is the virtual file system available within the application.

There are two main classes used; one is `IsolatedStorageSettings` class and other is `IsolatedStorageFile` class. Both classes are part of the **namespace** `System.IO.IsolatedStorage`.

`IsolatedStorageSettings` uses the dictionary mechanism to store data, hence it uses a key and a value pair for storing any value. Some of the most commonly used methods are `Add`, `Remove`, and `Contains`.

The `IsolatedStorageFile` class uses isolated storage with files and directories. Therefore, you can save any file stream to the local storage using `IsolatedStorageFileStream`. Some of the common methods used for managing the files are `FileExists`, `CreateFile`, `OpenFile`, and `DeleteFile`. Similarly, `DirectoryExists`, `CreateDirectory`, and `DeleteDirectory` are methods used for managing folders.

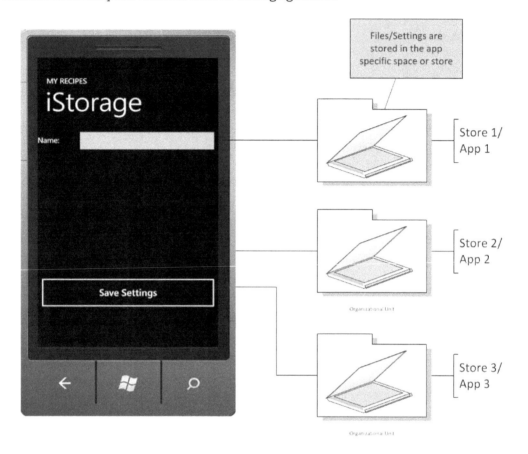

Saving user settings

In our first recipe, we will introduce the namespace and the classes used in isolated storage and also learn how to save simple user settings to local storage and retrieve the user settings from the local storage.

Getting ready

1. Open the Visual Studio for Phone 7 and create a Windows Phone Application. Name the application `Ch2_Recipe1` and click on **OK**.

2. After you open the project, press *F5* and run it to make sure everything compiles without errors.

How to do it...

Let's build a simple page to display a textbox, where one can enter a name and store it so it automatically appears each time this app is started.

1. Open the `MainPage.xaml` file and change the name of the application title and page title as follows:

```
<!--TitlePanel contains the name of the application and page
   title-->

<StackPanel x:Name="TitlePanel" Grid.Row="0"  Grid.ColumnSpan="2">
  <TextBlock x:Name="ApplicationTitle" Text="MY RECIPES"
    Style="{StaticResource PhoneTextNormalStyle}"/>
  <TextBlock x:Name="PageTitle" Text="iStorage"
    Style="{StaticResource PhoneTextTitle1Style}"/>
</StackPanel>
```

2. Press *F5* and see the results.

3. Let's add a `TextBlock` to display `Name`. In order to display two columns, we should change the `Grid ColumnDefinition` and `RowDefinition` as follows:

```
<!--LayoutRoot is the root grid where all page content is placed->
<Grid x:Name="LayoutRoot" Background="Transparent">
<Grid.RowDefinitions>
  <RowDefinition Height="Auto"/>
  <RowDefinition Height="*"/>
  <RowDefinition Height="*"/>
</Grid.RowDefinitions>

<Grid.ColumnDefinitions>
  <ColumnDefinition  Width="100">
  </ColumnDefinition>
  <ColumnDefinition>
  </ColumnDefinition>
</Grid.ColumnDefinitions>
```

4. Add one `TextBlock` and one `Textbox` element. Then we will add one `Button` element to save the settings:

```
<TextBlock x:Name ="tbName" Text ="Name:" Grid.Row="1"
  Margin="0,20,0,132" Grid.RowSpan="2" />
<TextBox x:Name ="tbNameContent"  Grid.ColumnSpan="2" Text =""
  Grid.Row="1" Grid.Column ="1" MaxHeight="100"
  VerticalAlignment="Top"/>
<Button x:Name="btnSaveSettings" Grid.Row="2" Grid.ColumnSpan="2"
  Content="Save Settings" MaxHeight="100"
  Click="btnSaveSettings_Click" />
```

5. Now open the `MainPage.xaml.cs` file and add the namespace `System.IO.IsolatedStorage`.

6. Define the `IsolatedStorageSettings` as `mySettings` as shown in the partial illustration of the `MainPage` class below:

```
public partial class MainPage : PhoneApplicationPage
{
   IsolatedStorageSettings mySettings;
   // Constructor
   public MainPage()
   {
       ……
```

7. In the `MainPage` constructor, we will create an instance of the `ApplicationSettings` object and call it `mySettings`:

```
mySettings = IsolatedStorageSettings.ApplicationSettings;
```

8. Now check if the local stored value `"setName"` exists. If true, then save the content to XAML element `tbNameContent`:

```
if (
   mySettings
   .Contains("setName"))
   tbNameContent.Text = mySettings
     ["setName"].ToString();
```

9. Add the `Save` button click event. Here we will first check if the text is empty or null using `String.IsNullOrEmpty`, and then either assign the text in `mySettings`, or use the `Add` method of `ApplicationSettings`:

```
private void btnSaveSettings_Click(object sender,
   RoutedEventArgs e)
{

   if (!String.IsNullOrEmpty(tbNameContent.Text))
   {
```

```
    if (mySettings.Contains("setName"))
    {
      mySettings["setName"] = tbNameContent.Text;
    }
    else
      mySettings.Add("setName", tbNameContent.Text);

    mySettings.Save();
  }
}
```

10. Press *F5*, type in a name in the textbox, and click on **Save Settings** as shown in the following screenshot. When you navigate away from the app and come back to the main page, you will still see the name you saved in the textbox.

How it works...

Isolated storage settings save the key and value pair in a dictionary file and it is then saved to the local store. We created the instance of the `ApplicationSettings` object first and then use the instance in all the methods within the `MainPage` class.

Also note that before reading from the key/value pair, we check if the key exists in the isolated storage.

There's more...

You can learn more about the isolated storage classes at the following MSDN address: `http://msdn.microsoft.com/en-us/library/ff769510(v=vs.92).aspx`.

Windows Phone 7.1 SDK comes with a command-line utility tool for exploring Isolated storage, which is called ISETool. This file is located in your local drive `C:\Program Files (x86)\ Microsoft SDKs\Windows Phone\v7.1\Tools\IsolatedStorageExplorerTool\ ISETool.exe`

See also

In the next recipe, we shall explore how to save using the file storage technique. Also, check the recipe *Saving username and password to a local store* in this chapter to understand how `ApplicationSettings` can be used to save multiple key/value pairs of information.

Opening and creating a file

In this recipe, we will learn how to open a file from local file storage and how to save the user settings to local file storage.

Getting ready

1. Open Visual Studio for Phone 7 and create a Windows Phone Application. Name the application `Ch2_Recipe2` and click on **OK**.

2. After you open the project, just press *F5* and run it to make sure you don't get any error.

How to do it...

Let's build a simple page with a textbox to enter text to save and a text block to display the saved text in the local file storage.

1. Open the `MainPage.xaml` file and change the application title and page title to `MY RECIPES` and `iFileStorage` respectively:

   ```
   <!--TitlePanel contains the name of the application and
     page title-->
   <StackPanel x:Name="TitlePanel" Grid.Row="0" Margin="12,17,0,28">
     <TextBlock x:Name="ApplicationTitle" Text="MY RECIPES"
       Style="{StaticResource PhoneTextNormalStyle}"/>
     <TextBlock x:Name="PageTitle" Text="iFileStorage" Margin="9,-
       7,0,0" Style="{StaticResource PhoneTextTitle1Style}"/>
   </StackPanel>
   ```

2. Next, add a text block and a textbox within the `ContentPanel` grid as follows:

   ```
   <TextBlock x:Name ="tbName" Text ="Name:" Grid.Row="1"
     Grid.Column ="0"/>
   <TextBox x:Name ="tbNameContent"  Grid.ColumnSpan="2" Text =""
     Grid.Row="1" Grid.Column ="1" MaxHeight="100"
     VerticalAlignment="Top"/>
   ```

3. Now let's add a `TextBlock` with the name `tbFileStored` to display what was stored in the file:

   ```
   <TextBlock x:Name ="tbStoredNames" Text ="Stored File:"
     Grid.Row="2" Grid.Column ="0"/>
   <TextBlock x:Name ="tbStoredNamesList" Text ="" Grid.Row="2"
     Grid.Column ="1"/>
   ```

4. Open the `MainPage.xaml.cs` file and add the following two namespaces:

   ```
   using System.IO.IsolatedStorage;
   using System.IO;
   ```

5. Add a string constant to store the name of the file. We will save it in the local storage. For this recipe we will use the name `myfile1.txt`:

   ```
   const string FILENAME = "myfile1.txt";
   ```

6. Now we shall add a method to open the file from the local storage and display it in our text block:

   ```
   private void ReadFromFile()
   {
     using(var localStore =
       IsolatedStorageFile.GetUserStoreForApplication())
     {
       //check if the file exists
   ```

```
if (localStore.FileExists(FILENAME))
{
  //using the stream reader class open the file
  using (StreamReader sr = new
    StreamReader(localStore.OpenFile(FILENAME,
     FileMode.Open, FileAccess.Read)))
  {
    //just assign to the Text Block
    tbFileStored.Text = sr.ReadToEnd();
  }
}
else //if there is no file found
  tbFileStored.Text = "No Data Stored";

  }
}
```

7. Now that we have a method to open the file and display it, let's call this in the `MainPage` constructor as shown in the partial code snippet below:

```
// Constructor
public MainPage()
{
  InitializeComponent();
  ReadFromFile();
  ...
```

8. Press *F5* and run; you will see **No Data Stored**, as shown in the following screenshot. This is because we didn't save anything in the local storage.

10. Now add a button with the name `btnSaveToFile`. When you select the `Click` property of the button in the XAML, you will get an option to create a new event method; name it `btnSaveToFile_Click`:

```
<Button x:Name="btnSaveToFile" Grid.Row="3" Grid.ColumnSpan="2"
   Content="Save Settings To A File" MaxHeight="100"
   Click="btnSaveToFile_Click" />
```

11. Now go to `MainPage.xaml.cs`, and add the following code to save the file to `btnSaveToFile_Click`:

```
private void btnSaveToFile_Click(object sender, RoutedEventArgs e)
{
  using(var localStore =
    IsolatedStorageFile.GetUserStoreForApplication())
  {
    //using the StreamWriter class, open the file if it already
      exists if not create a new file

    using (StreamWriter sw = new
      StreamWriter(localStore.OpenFile(FILENAME,
      FileMode.OpenOrCreate, FileAccess.Write)))
    {
      // let's load the file read into our text block
      sw.WriteLine(tbNameContent.Text);
    }
  }
  // now call the ReadFromFile method to display the
    content of the file
  ReadFromFile();
}
```

12. Press *F5* and run. Now type in some text in the **Name** textbox and click on the **Save Settings To A File** button. Now you should see the saved name in the `textblock` **Stored File**.

How it works...

In order to read from the file storage, we first check if the file exists in the storage. If it exists then we open it to read it, otherwise we create a file in the root folder.

Once the file is opened for reading, we use the `ReadToEnd` method to load the content of the text file to the text block.

In order to save the file to storage we perform similar steps to reading the file, but we use the `StreamWriter` class to open the file in write mode and then we use the `WriteLine` method to write it to the storage file.

There's more...

You can learn more about the `IsolatedStorageFile` classes at the following MSDN address: `http://msdn.microsoft.com/en-us/library/ff626519(v=VS.92).aspx`.

See also

In the recipe titled *Saving a background image to local storage* in this chapter, we will learn how to save an image or picture to isolated storage. Also, check *Chapter 3, XML as a Data Store*, to learn how to serialize and deserialize objects to local XML files.

Saving username and password to a local store

In this recipe we will learn how to save a username and password to local storage settings.

Getting ready

For this recipe let's copy the simple `MyTasks` app solution folder we built in *Chapter 1, Data Binding to UI Elements*, and rename the folder to `Ch2_Recipe3_MyTasks`. After you open the project, just press *F5* and run it to make sure you don't get any errors.

How to do it...

Let's add another icon in the bottom navigation bar to link it to the **Settings** page. Then create the **Settings** page with the different controls to save the username and password.

1. First, add another bar item at the bottom to navigate to user settings page, which we will be creating in step 3:

```xml
<!--Sample code showing usage of ApplicationBar-->
<phone:PhoneApplicationPage.ApplicationBar>
  <shell:ApplicationBar BackgroundColor="Orange"
    IsVisible="True" IsMenuEnabled="True">

      <shell:ApplicationBarIconButton
        IconUri="/Images/appbar.folder.rest.png"
        Click="ButtonFolder_Click" Text="Task Folder"/>

      <shell:ApplicationBarIconButton
        IconUri="/Images/appbar.add.rest.png"
        Click="ButtonAdd_Click" Text="Add Task"/>

      <!-- Add settings item for another icon for settings also
        create click event -->
      <shell:ApplicationBarIconButton
        IconUri="/Images/appbar.feature.settings.rest.png"
        Click="ButtonSettings_Click" Text="Picture"/>
  </shell:ApplicationBar>
</phone:PhoneApplicationPage.ApplicationBar>
```

2. Add the code to navigate to the new settings page:

```csharp
private void ButtonSettings_Click(object sender, EventArgs e)
{
  NavigationService.Navigate(new Uri("/Settings.xaml",
    UriKind.Relative));
}
```

3. Press *F5* and you should see the following page with the settings icon in the navigation bar:

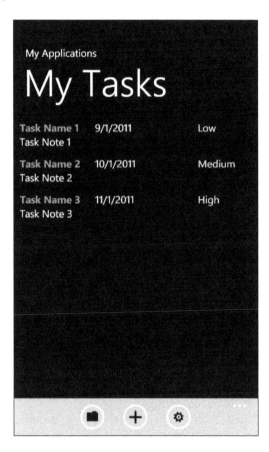

4. Right-click on the project in the **Solution Explorer** and select **Add New Item** to create a new phone page. Name the page `Settings.xaml`. In this page, add three textbox controls for collecting username, password, and confirmation password as shown in the following XAML.

```
<!--LayoutRoot is the root grid where all page content
  is placed-->
<Grid x:Name="LayoutRoot" Background="Transparent">
```

```xml
<Grid.RowDefinitions>
  <RowDefinition Height="Auto"/>
  <RowDefinition Height="*"/>
</Grid.RowDefinitions>
<!--TitlePanel contains the name of the application
  and page title-->
<StackPanel x:Name="TitlePanel" Grid.Row="0"
  Margin="12,17,0,28">
<TextBlock x:Name="ApplicationTitle" Text=
  "MY APPLICATION" Style="{StaticResource
  PhoneTextNormalStyle}"/>
<TextBlock x:Name="PageTitle" Text="App Settings"
  Margin="9,-7,0,0" Style="{StaticResource
  PhoneTextTitle1Style}"/>
</StackPanel>

<!--ContentPanel - place additional content here-->
<Grid x:Name="ContentPanel" Grid.Row="1" Margin="12,0,12,0">
  <TextBlock x:Name="tbUserName" HorizontalAlignment="Left"
    Height="30" Margin="8,16,0,0" TextWrapping="Wrap"
    Text="Username" VerticalAlignment="Top" Width="115"
    RenderTransformOrigin="0.498,0.55"/>

  <TextBlock x:Name="tbPassword" HorizontalAlignment="Left"
    Height="30" Margin="8,70,0,0" TextWrapping="Wrap"
    Text="Password" VerticalAlignment="Top" Width="115"/>

  <TextBox x:Name="txtUserName" Height="70" Margin=
    "119,0,70,0" VerticalAlignment="Top"/>

  <PasswordBox x:Name="txtPassword" Height="70"
    Margin="119,62,70,0"  VerticalAlignment="Top"/>

  <TextBlock Height="30" HorizontalAlignment="Left"
    Margin="12,138,0,0" Name="tbConfirm" Text="Confirm"
    TextWrapping="Wrap" VerticalAlignment="Top" Width="115" />

  <PasswordBox Height="70" Margin="119,123,70,0"
    Name="txtPasswordConfirm" VerticalAlignment="Top" />

  <Button x:Name="btnSave" Content="Save" Height="69"
    Margin="119,0,217,353" VerticalAlignment="Bottom"
    RenderTransformOrigin="0.969,0.514" Click="btnAdd_Click" />

  <Button x:Name="btnCancel" Content="Go Back"
    HorizontalAlignment="Right" Height="69" Margin="0,0,70,353"
    VerticalAlignment="Bottom" Width="145"
    Click="btnCancel_Click" />
</Grid>
</Grid>
```

5. Now let's add reference with the `using` statement for `System.IO.IsolatedStorage` in the `Settings.xaml.cs` file:

```
using System.IO.IsolatedStorage;
```

6. Create an instance of `IsolatedStorageSettings` and name it `mySettings`:

```
public partial class Settings : PhoneApplicationPage
{
  IsolatedStorageSettings mySettings;
  public Settings()
  …
```

7. Add the following code in the constructor:

```
public Settings()
{
  InitializeComponent();
  //Initialize the settings
  mySettings = IsolatedStorageSettings.ApplicationSettings;

  // Display settings stored in the local storage for setUserName
    if (mySettings.Contains("setUserName"))
      txtUserName.Text = mySettings["setUserName"].ToString();

  // Display settings stored in the local storage for setPassword
    if (mySettings.Contains("setPassword"))
      txtPassword.Password = mySettings["setPassword"].ToString();
}
```

8. Add the event click method. Here we will validate if the **Password** text matches the **Confirm** text. Then we will either save or add the settings fields, as follows:

```
private void btnAdd_Click(object sender, RoutedEventArgs e)
{
  if (txtUserName.Text != "" && txtPassword.Password != "")
  {
    if (txtPassword.Password == txtPasswordConfirm.Password)
    {
      if (mySettings.Contains("setUserName"))
      {
        mySettings["setUserName"] = txtUserName.Text;
      }
      else
      mySettings.Add("setUserName", txtUserName.Text);

      if (mySettings.Contains("setPassword"))
      {
        mySettings["setPassword"] = txtPassword.Password;
      }
```

```
        else
          mySettings.Add("setPassword", txtPassword.Password);

          mySettings.Save();

          MessageBox.Show("Settings Saved Successfully");
      }
      else
        MessageBox.Show("Passwords are not matching");
    }
}
```

9. Add the cancel button event method. In this method we just navigate back to the main page:

```
private void btnCancel_Click(object sender, RoutedEventArgs e)
{
  NavigationService.GoBack();
}
```

10. Press *F5* and type in a username and password. Click on **Save**. Now all the information is saved. Just navigate away from the **Settings** page and then come back to the **Settings** page. You should see the saved username and password.

How it works...

Saving username and password follows a concept similar to the recipe *Saving User Settings* in this chapter.

Here we use the `IsolatedStorageSettings.ApplicationSettings` class to store and retrieve. We create the instance of the `ApplicationSettings` in the beginning of the class and then we use this instance for both writing and reading.

Settings are saved as key-value pairs in a dictionary. We check if the setting's name exists, if it does, then we set the value to the key, otherwise we add the key and value pair to create a new one.

When the save button event is triggered, we check if the password and the confirm password match, otherwise an error is displayed and we are asked to enter the password again. If the passwords match, then we set the values to `ApplicationSettings` either using the `Add` method or assigning the value to the key. Essentially, we save both username and password information locally for later retrieval.

There's more...

In this recipe you learned how to save multiple data fields in the local settings. You can use the locally stored settings to remove the requirement from users to enter the same information again and again. For example, you can use the username and password information to login automatically to an online service to download information at a regular interval. Also, you can save an object to application settings and then databind to XAML controls using datacontext.

See also

Check the *Saving User Settings* recipe in this chapter, which also covers how to save user settings.

Saving a background image to local storage

In this recipe we will learn how to save image files to a local storage folder. We will make use of the `IsolatedStorageFile` class.

Getting ready

For this recipe let's copy the simple `MyTasks` app solution folder we built in the previous recipe and rename the folder to `Ch2_Recipe4_MyTasks`. After you open the project, just press *F5* and run it to make sure you don't get any errors.

How to do it...

Let's add a button control in the settings page to launch the built-in Photo Chooser utility. Once the desired photo is selected we will save the image to local storage.

1. Open the settings `.xaml` file and add a text block control and button control inside the `ContentPanel` grid:

   ```
   <TextBlock Height="55" HorizontalAlignment="Left"
     Margin="12,199,0,0" Name="textBlock1" Text="Bacground Image"
     TextWrapping="Wrap" VerticalAlignment="Top" Width="115" />
   <Button Content="Browse" Height="77" Margin="119,0,70,331"
     Name="btnBrowse" VerticalAlignment="Bottom"
     Click="btnBrowse_Click" />
   ```

2. Open the `settings.xaml.cs` file and add the following two `using` statements:

   ```
   using System.Windows.Media.Imaging;
   using Microsoft.Phone.Tasks;
   ```

3. Let's create an instance of `PhotoChooserTask`, which will let us pick photos using Photo Chooser. Add the following code before the `Settings` constructor:

   ```
   private PhotoChooserTask bkPhotoTask;
   ```

4. Add the following code inside the `Settings` constructor to initialize `PhotoChooserTask` and then the photo task completed event handler in the `Settings` constructor:

   ```
   // initialize PhotoChooserTask
   bkPhotoTask = new PhotoChooserTask();

   // add an event
   bkPhotoTask.Completed += new
     EventHandler<PhotoResult>(bkPhotoTask_Completed);
   ```

5. In the button event click method, call the `PhotoTask.Show` method to launch the Photo Chooser. After the photo is selected, the `PhotoTask_Completed` event is triggered, which calls the method `bkPhotoTask_Completed`. This method saves the selected image to the `BitmapImage` stream:

   ```
   private void btnBrowse_Click(object sender,RoutedEventArgs e)
   {
     bkPhotoTask.Show();
   }

   private void bkPhotoTask_Completed(object sender, PhotoResult e)
   {
     if (e.TaskResult == TaskResult.OK)
     {
   ```

```
      BitmapImage bkImage = new BitmapImage();
      bkImage.SetSource(e.ChosenPhoto);
      // save the image to local storage
      SaveImageToLocalStorage(bkImage);
  }
}
```

6. Add the saved image stream to an isolated storage file. Here the `Imaging Extension` class is used to encode the image into the `JPEG` image stream. Then the image is set to app background:

```
// save the image to local storage
private void SaveImageToLocalStorage(BitmapImage bkImage)
{

  using(IsolatedStorageFile isFile =
    IsolatedStorageFile.GetUserStoreForApplication())
  {

    WriteableBitmap wImage = new WriteableBitmap(bkImage);

    if(!isFile.DirectoryExists("Images"))
    {
      isFile.CreateDirectory("Images");
    }

    using(IsolatedStorageFileStream imageStream =
      isFile.OpenFile(@"Images\bkgroundImage.jpg",
      System.IO.FileMode.OpenOrCreate))
    {

    Extensions.SaveJpeg(wImage, imageStream,
      wImage.PixelWidth, wImage.PixelHeight, 0, 100);
    }

    var app = Application.Current as App;
    if (app == null)
      return;
    var imageBrush = new ImageBrush { ImageSource   = bkImage,
      Opacity = 0.5d };

    app.RootFrame.Background = imageBrush;

  }
}
```

7. Press *F5* and navigate to the **Settings** page. Click on the **Browse** button. This will launch the Photo Chooser:

8. In the Photo Chooser, you should be able to see all the albums in your phone. Pick the album:

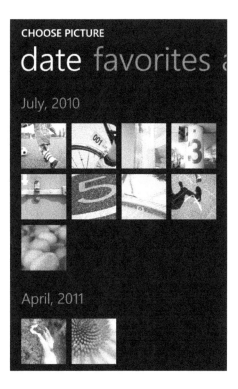

9. Now pick a photo to make it your background. After you select the picture, `PhotoChooserTask` confirms that **Settings Saved Successfully**. Click on **ok** to close the message box.

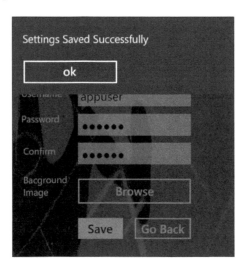

10. As we apply the image application background brush, the **Settings** page background will display the selected photo. Now you can navigate back to the main page. You should see the selected photo as the background image.

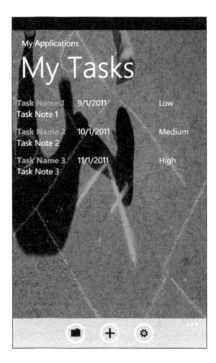

How it works...

In order to save the image to local store, we use the `IsolatedStorageFile` class. We first create the `Images` folder.

Using the `IsolatedStorageFileStream` we open the image file chosen for the background image. We use the `FileMode` as `OpenOrCreate`. If it already exists, then it just opens, otherwise the image is saved to the file stream using the `SaveJpeg` method of the `Extensions` class.

There's more...

In this recipe, we explored how to save images and create folders. You can learn more about files and folders at the following MSDN address:
`http://msdn.microsoft.com/en-us/library/ff626519%28v=VS.92%29.aspx`.

See also

Read the *Opening and creating a file* recipe in this chapter to understand more on `Opening` and `Creating` files in local storage. Also, in *Chapter 5, Using On-Device Databases*, we will learn how to use the on-device databases as another option to save information locally.

3
XML as a Data Store

In this chapter, we will cover:

- ▶ Opening a local XML file
- ▶ Opening a remote XML file
- ▶ Navigating the XML file to search
- ▶ Object serialization to XML

Introduction

XML is the most popular open standard format for exchanging information in today's world. XML is human and machine readable. We don't go into detail about XML theory in this chapter, but if you want a better understanding on this topic you can refer to the online resource at `http://www.w3.org/standards/xml/`.

XML can be parsed using two different methods. The first method is using **LINQ to XML**, and the second method is using **XmlReader**. XmlReader is used for reading many documents or large documents that have the same structure. On the other hand, if you are reading a different structured XML, you can use LINQ to XML. XmlReader can be used for forward-only and read-only situations. If we need to write or create XML content, then the `XmlWriter` class is used. Caution should be exercised as large documents can take up significant resources and memory that can slow the response time of the application.

LINQ to XML is an interface supported in the **WP7** (**Windows Phone 7**) for reading, editing, and deleting XML documents. This is similar to XML parsers. LINQ to XML is generally used for smaller documents.

XML is used indifferent ways in WP7 application development; here are a few scenarios:

1. XAML is the XML format specific to the user interface. All the user elements are represented in the XML tags.

2. XML is used for saving the settings or caching any information to local storage..

3. Object serialization formats objects into an XML file.

4. OData (Open Data Protocol), which is discussed in the *Chapter 4, Using Open Data*, returns the query results in XML format.

5. **REST** (**REpresentational State Transfer**) web services return the data in XML format.

Opening a local XML file

In this recipe let's try to open an XML file saved in the local application folder. We will make use of the XDocument parse method for opening the XML file. LINQ to XML is the best and the easiest way to navigate the XML for Silverlight applications. LINQ to XML replaced the XSLT transformation in C#.

Getting ready

For this recipe let's create a new project named `Recipe1_LinqToXml` under the solution folder named `Ch3_Recipes`. We will use this solution for all our samples in this chapter. Change the Application Name in the `MainPage.xaml` to `LINQToXML`. Press *F5* and run to make sure you have no errors.

How to do it...

In the following steps we will create an XML file with sample data for our testing purposes and then we will load the results of the LINQ to SQL query into a list box control to be displayed on the screen.

1. Open the `MainPage.xaml.cs` file and add the assembly reference for accessing isolated storage, which is `System.IO.IsolatedStorage`. As we are going to use XML and LINQ, we will first add the references to `System.Xml` and `System.Xml.Linq` in the project and then include the XML and LINQ namespace using declaratives as shown in the following code snippet:

   ```
   using System.IO.IsolatedStorage;
   using System.Xml;
   using System.Xml.Linq;
   ```

2. Similar to the `Ch2_MyTasks` recipe sample, let's copy or include `DataClass.cs`. Make sure to change the namespace to `Recipe1_LinqToXml`.

3. Let's create a sample `XML` file with sample data and call it `MyTasks.xml`, as follows:

```
<?xmlversion="1.0"encoding="utf-8" ?>
<tasks>
  <taskname="name 1" notes="notes 1" priority="Low"
    datedue="03/01/2011" datecreated="02/01/2011"/>


  <taskname="name 2" notes="notes 2" priority="High"
    datedue="04/01/2011" datecreated="02/01/2011"/>


  <taskname="name 3" notes="notes 3" priority="Medium"
    datedue="05/01/2011" datecreated="02/01/2011"/>
</tasks>
```

4. Select `MyTasks.xml`, and in the **Properties** make sure **Build Action** is set to **Content** and **Copy to Output** is set to **Copy if newer** as shown in the following screenshot:

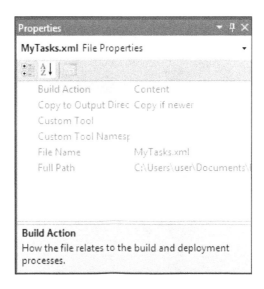

5. Open the `MainPage.xaml.cs` file. Add a new method named `parseXMLUsingLinq` with a string parameter `passedXmlFileName` to open the file from the local folder and parse the XML file:

```
private void parseXMLUsingLinq(stringpassedXmlFileName)
{
  XDocumentxdoc = XDocument.Load(passedXmlFileName);
  IEnumerable<DataClass>iTasks;

  iTasks = from task inxdoc.Descendants("task")
  select new DataClass
```

```
      {
        Name = (string)task.Attribute("name"),
        Notes = (string)task.Attribute("notes"),
        Priority = (string)task.Attribute("priority"),
        DateDue = (DateTime)task.Attribute("datedue"),
        DateCreated = (DateTime)task.Attribute("datecreated")
      };
      lstTasks.ItemsSource = iTasks;
   }
```

6. Now add the `MainPage_Loaded` event method and call the `parseXMLUsingLinq` method passing the name of the XML file we created:

```
private void MainPage_Loaded(object sender, RoutedEventArgs e)
{
   parseXMLUsingLinq("MyTasks.xml");
}
```

7. Press *F5*. Now you will see the results, as shown in the following screenshot:

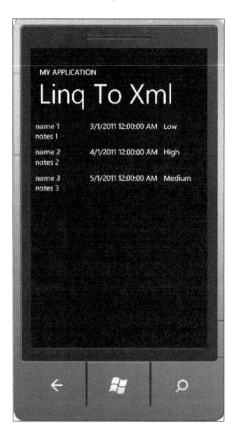

How it works...

In this recipe we opened the XML file from the local storage using the parse method of the XDocument class and bound it to the list box control. We initially loaded the XML content into XDocument and used the LINQ statement to get all the task elements.

There's more...

In this recipe we learned how to open a local XML file. We can learn more in the following section using the XmlReader instead of LINQ to XML. Also, refer to the following MSDN article to learn more on the subject of LINQ to SQL:
http://msdn.microsoft.com/en-us/library/bb425822.aspx

Parsing XML using the XmlReader class

Now let's try parsing the same XML using the XmlReader. Add a new project to the previous solution Ch3_Recipes and call it Recipe2_XmlReader. Copy the DataClass.cs and MyTasks.xml files from the previous recipe and add them to the project. Change the Namespace in the DataClass.cs file and run it to make sure everything compiles successfully.

1. Open the MainPage.xaml.cs file and add another method called parseXMLUsingReader with parameter StringpassedXmlFileName.

```
private void parseXMLUsingReader(stringReaderpassedXmlFileName)
{

    XmlReaderrdr=XmlReader.Create(passedXmlContent);

    while (rdr.Read())
    {
      if (rdr.NodeType == XmlNodeType.Element)
      {
        if (rdr.Name == "task")
        {
          DataClass task = new DataClass
          {
            Name = rdr["name"],
            Notes = rdr["notes"],
            Priority = rdr["priority"],
            DateCreated = Convert.ToDateTime(rdr["datecreated"]),
            DateDue=  Convert.ToDateTime(rdr["datedue"])
          };
        }
      }
    }
}
```

2. Let's add the `MainPage_Loaded` event in the `MainPage.xaml` file at the last line as `Loaded="MainPage_Loaded"`, as shown in the following code snippet:

```
<phone:PhoneApplicationPage
x:Class="Recipe2_XmlReader.MainPage"
xmlns="http://schemas.microsoft.com/winfx/2006/xaml/presentation"
xmlns:x=http://schemas.microsoft.com/winfx/2006/xaml
  xmlns:phone="clr-namespace:Microsoft.Phone.Controls;
assembly=Microsoft.Phone"
  xmlns:shell="clr-namespace:Microsoft.Phone.Shell;
assembly=Microsoft.Phone"
xmlns:d="http://schemas.microsoft.com/expression/blend/2008"
xmlns:mc="http://schemas.openxmlformats.org/markup-
compatibility/2006"
mc:Ignorable="d" d:DesignWidth="480" d:DesignHeight="768"
FontFamily="{StaticResourcePhoneFontFamilyNormal}"
FontSize="{StaticResourcePhoneFontSizeNormal}"
 Foreground="{StaticResourcePhoneForegroundBrush}"
SupportedOrientations="Portrait" Orientation="Portrait"
shell:SystemTray.IsVisible="True" Loaded="MainPage_Loaded">
```

3. In the `MainPage_Loaded` event method call `parseXMLUsingReader` with `"MyTasks.xml"` as the parameter:

```
private void MainPage_Loaded(object sender, RoutedEventArgs e)
{
  parseXMLUsingReader("MyTasks.xml");
}
```

4. Press *F5*. The results should be as shown in the following screenshot:

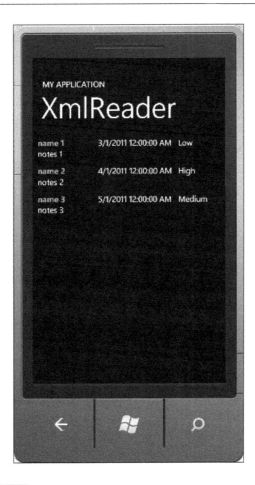

See also

Check the recipe *Navigate the XML file* to understand how to parse the XML file and search for specific strings in it. Also, check the recipe *Opening a remote XML file*.

Navigating the XML file

In this recipe, let's look more into navigating the XML file. There are many ways to navigate. Here we will learn how to load the XML file directly and find specific information and return it using LINQ methods.

Let's add a new project called `Recipe4_SearchXml` to our `Ch3_Recipes` solution. Copy `DataClass.cs` and `MyTasks.xml` from the first recipe. Change the name of the page to `SearchXml`.

In the following steps, let's create an application to get the priority of a task by navigating the XML document:

1. Let's use the `MyTasks.xml` we created earlier:

   ```xml
   <?xmlversion="1.0"encoding="utf-8" ?>
   <tasks>
     <taskname="name 1" notes="notes 1" priority="Low"
       datedue="03/01/2011" datecreated="02/01/2011"/>

     <taskname="name 2" notes="notes 2" priority="High"
       datedue="04/01/2011" datecreated="02/01/2011"/>

     <taskname="name 3" notes="notes 3" priority="Medium"
       datedue="05/01/2011" datecreated="02/01/2011"/>
   </tasks>
   ```

2. In the XML file, we have each task as a child element under the parent element **tasks**. Each task element has attributes **name**, **notes**, **priority**, **datedue**, and **datecreated**.

3. Add a `TextBox` control to search the name of the task and a `Button` control inside the `ContentPanel` grid:

   ```xml
   <Grid x:Name="ContentPanel" Grid.Row="1"
     Margin="12,0" Grid.ColumnSpan="2">

     <TextBox Height="72" HorizontalAlignment="Left" Margin="0,52,0,0"
       Name="textBox1" Text="" VerticalAlignment="Top" Width="460" />

     <TextBlock Height="30" HorizontalAlignment="Left"
       Margin="14,32,0,0" Name="textBlock1" Text="Search Task
       Name" VerticalAlignment="Top" />

     <Button Content="Get Priority"
       Height="72" HorizontalAlignment="Left" Margin="0,116,0,0"
       Name="button1" VerticalAlignment="Top" Width="197"
       Click="button1_Click" />
   </Grid>
   ```

4. Add another `TextBlock` to display the results found in the search:

```xml
<Grid x:Name=" ContentPane2" Grid.Row="1"
  Margin="12,216,12,0" Grid.ColumnSpan="2">

  <TextBlock Height="156" HorizontalAlignment="Left"
    Margin="14,32,0,0" Name="txbResults" Text="search
    results" VerticalAlignment="Top" Width="425"FontSize="56" />

</Grid>
```

5. Open the `MainPage.xaml.cs` file and add a method named `getPriority` with a parameter as the task name:

```csharp
// Sample showing how to navigate to a specific
// node of the xml document
Private string getPriority(stringtaskName)
{
    XDocument doc = XDocument.Load(@"MyTasks.xml");

    var tasks = doc.Document.Descendants(XName.Get("task"));

    string priority = null;

    foreach (var task in tasks)
    {
        if (task.Attribute(XName.Get("name")).Value == taskName)
        {
            priority = task.Attribute(XName.Get("priority")).Value;
        }
    }

    return priority;
}
```

6. Call the `getPriority` method when the search button is clicked:

```csharp
Private void button1_Click(object sender, RoutedEventArgs e)
{
    StringtxtSearch = textBox1.Text;

    this.txbResults.Text = getPriority(txtSearch);

}
```

7. Press *F5*. Now search for task name **name1** and you should get the result **Low** as the priority, as illustrated in the following screenshot:

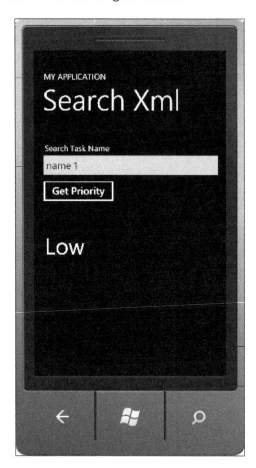

How it works...

First we use the XDocument to load the XML file MyTasks.xml to a local variable. Then, we get all the task child elements using the Descendants method. We loop through each of the task child elements and compare the attributes. If the name matches the **Task Name** we are looking for, then the **Get Priority** attribute value is returned.

There's more...

For navigating the XML, we can also use the XPath language and XPathNavigator classes. For more information on this topic refer to MSDN:

http://msdn.microsoft.com/en-us/library/0ysh8kd0(v=vs.80).aspx

Check the recipe titled *Object serialization to XML* in this chapter to understand how you can serialize and deserialize objects to and from XML file.

Opening a remote XML file

In the first recipe *Opening a local XML file*, we opened an XML file from the local folder; now let's try opening an XML file from a remote location.

Getting ready

1. Create a new project called `Recipe3_RemoteXml` under `Ch3_Recipes`.

2. Open your local **IIS (Internet Information Services)** root folder and copy the XML file `MyTasks.xml` we created in the preceding recipe.

3. You can also host this file in any remote server, which can be accessed using a simple URI. For this recipe, let's copy the XML file to localhost's root folder. You can learn more on how to install the IIS on your machine using this link: `http://learn.iis.net/page.aspx/28/installing-iis-7-on-windows-vista-and-windows-7/`.

4. Navigate to the file using the browser and the following link `http://localhost/mytasks.xml`. It should look like the following screenshot:

```xml
<?xml version="1.0" encoding="utf-8" ?>
<tasks>
    <task name="name 1" notes="notes 1" priority="Low" datedue="03/01/2011"
        datecreated="02/01/2011" />
    <task name="name 2" notes="notes 2" priority="High" datedue="04/01/2011"
        datecreated="02/01/2011" />
    <task name="name 3" notes="notes 3" priority="Medium" datedue="05/01/2011"
        datecreated="02/01/2011" />
</tasks>
```

How to do it...

In the following steps, we will create a form to collect the remote XML file location information in a textbox control, and then using the `WebClient` class we will download the file. Once the file download is completed, we will display it in the list box control.

1. Open the `MainPage.xaml` file and rename the app to `RemoteXML`.

2. Add a `TextBox` control to collect the remote XML file and a `Button` control inside the `ContentPanel` grid:

```
<!--TitlePanel contains the name of the application and
  page title-->
<StackPanel x:Name="TitlePanel"Grid.Row="0" Margin="12,17,0,28">
  <TextBlock x:Name="ApplicationTitle" Text="MY APPLICATION"
    Style="{StaticResourcePhoneTextNormalStyle}"/>
  <TextBlock x:Name="PageTitle" Text="Remote Xml"
    Margin="9,-7,0,0" Style="{StaticResource
    PhoneTextTitle1Style}"/>
</StackPanel>

<!--ContentPanel - place additional content here-->
<Grid x:Name="ContentPanel"Grid.Row="1" Margin="12,0,12,0">
  <TextBox Height="72"HorizontalAlignment="Left" Margin="0,52,0,0"
    Name="textBox1" Text=""VerticalAlignment="Top" Width="460" />
  <TextBlock Height="30"HorizontalAlignment="Left"
    Margin="14,32,0,0" Name="textBlock1" Text="Remote Xml File
    Location:"VerticalAlignment="Top" />
  <Button Content="Go" Height="72"HorizontalAlignment="Left"
    Margin="0,116,0,0" Name="button1"VerticalAlignment="Top"
    Width="160" Click="button1_Click" />
</Grid>
```

3. Now add another `Grid` following the preceding grid to display the result just like we did in the preceding recipe:

```
<!--ContentPanel - place additional content here-->
<Grid x:Name="ContentPanel2" Margin="12,217,12,-13"Grid.Row="1">
  <ListBox x:Name ="lstTasks" Margin="0,6,0,0">
    <ListBox.ItemTemplate>
      <DataTemplate>
        <Grid>
          <Grid.RowDefinitions>
            <RowDefinition />
            <RowDefinition />
            <RowDefinition Height="15" />
          </Grid.RowDefinitions>

          <Grid.ColumnDefinitions>
            <ColumnDefinition Width="150" />
            <ColumnDefinition Width="200" />
```

```xml
        <ColumnDefinition Width="100" />
      </Grid.ColumnDefinitions>

      <TextBlockGrid.Row="0"Grid.Column="0" Text="{Binding
        Name}"FontWeight="Bold" Foreground="OrangeRed"/>

      <TextBlockGrid.Row="0"Grid.Column="1"
        Text="{BindingDateDue}" />

      <TextBlockGrid.Row="0"Grid.Column="2"
        Text="{Binding Priority}" Foreground="Yellow"/>

      <TextBlockGrid.Row="1"Grid.ColumnSpan="3"
        Text="{Binding Notes}" />

      <TextBlockGrid.Row="2"Grid.ColumnSpan="3" />

      </Grid>
    </DataTemplate>
  </ListBox.ItemTemplate>
</ListBox>
</Grid>
```

4. Now open the `MainPage.xaml.cs` file and add the following lines of code to download the XML file from the remote location using the `WebClient` class:

```csharp
WebClientremoteXml;

PublicMainPage()
{
  InitializeComponent();
  remoteXml = new WebClient();
  remoteXml.DownloadStringCompleted +=
    new DownloadStringCompletedEventHandler
    (remoteXml_DownloadStringCompleted);

}
```

5. Add the event handler method `remoteXml_DownloadStringCompleted`, which parses the XML document:

```csharp
Private void remoteXml_DownloadStringCompleted(object sender,
  DownloadStringCompletedEventArgs e)
{
  XDocumentxdoc = XDocument.Parse(e.Result);
  IEnumerable<DataClass>iTasks;

  iTasks = from task inxdoc.Descendants("task")
  selectnewDataClass
  {
    Name = (string)task.Attribute("name"),
```

```
        Notes = (string)task.Attribute("notes"),
        Priority = (string)task.Attribute("priority"),
        DateDue = (DateTime)task.Attribute("datedue"),
        DateCreated = (DateTime)task.Attribute("datecreated")
    };

    lstTasks.ItemsSource = iTasks;
}
```

6. Now let's add the button click event method. Here we format the URI text in the textbox control to `Uri` and then call the `DownloadStringAsync` method to fetch the XML file from the remote location:

```
private void button1_Click(object sender, RoutedEventArgs e)
{

    stringtxtUri = textBox1.Text;
    txtUri = Uri.EscapeUriString(txtUri);
    Uriuri = newUri(txtUri);
    remoteXml.DownloadStringAsync(uri);
}
```

7. Press *F5* and type in the URL of the `MyTasks.xml` file. When you click on **Go,** you should see the parsed XML content displayed in the list box control, as shown in the following screenshot:

How it works...

We first declared `WebClient` and then added the event handler. Using `WebClient` is the easiest way to access remote files. As it is asynchronous, we have to wait for the download to complete. We added the download event handler.

In the button click event method, we converted the text from the textbox to escape the Uri string. Then, we got all the task child elements using the `Descendants` method. Finally, the resulting list was bound to the list box control.

There's more...

We can add more features like saving the XML file to local storage or saving the URI string to our local storage settings file. Refer to MSDN for more information on LINQ to XML at the following link:

`http://msdn.microsoft.com/en-us/library/bb425822.aspx`.

See also

Check *Chapter 6*, *Representational State Transfer*, to understand more on how REST-style web services work.

Object serialization to XML

In this recipe, we shall explore how to serialize an object and then deserialize the XML back to an object.

Getting ready

Open a new Phone 7 application project and save it as `Recipe5_SerializeXml`. Press *F5* and make sure it compiles without any errors.

How to do it...

In the following steps, we will create sample data to save and serialize it to XML. We will then open it using the deserialize method and then display it in a list box.

1. Open the `MainPage.xaml` file; add a button to trigger the saving and opening of the serialization. The XAML should look like the following code snippet:

    ```
    <Grid x:Name="LayoutRoot" Background="Transparent">
      <Grid.RowDefinitions>
        <RowDefinition Height="Auto"/>
        <RowDefinition Height="*"/>
    ```

```xml
        </Grid.RowDefinitions>

    <!--TitlePanel contains the name of the application and
      page title-->
    <StackPanel x:Name="TitlePanel" Grid.Row="0"
      Margin="12,17,0,28">

      <TextBlock x:Name="ApplicationTitle" Text="MY APPLICATION"
        Style="{StaticResourcePhoneTextNormalStyle}"/>

      <TextBlock x:Name="PageTitle" Text="Serialize Xml"
        Margin="9,-7,0,0" Style="{StaticResource
        PhoneTextTitle1Style}"/>

    </StackPanel>

    <!--ContentPanel - place additional content here-->
    <Grid x:Name="ContentPanel" Margin="12,146,12,0" Grid.Row="1">
      <Grid.ColumnDefinitions>
        <ColumnDefinition Width="213*" />
        <ColumnDefinition Width="243*" />
      </Grid.ColumnDefinitions>

      <ListBox x:Name ="lstTasks"
        Margin="0,6,0,198" Grid.ColumnSpan="2">
        <ListBox.ItemTemplate>
          <DataTemplate>
            <Grid>
              <Grid.RowDefinitions>
                <RowDefinition />
                <RowDefinition />
                <RowDefinition Height="15" />
              </Grid.RowDefinitions>

              <Grid.ColumnDefinitions>
                <ColumnDefinition Width="150" />
                <ColumnDefinition Width="200" />
                <ColumnDefinition Width="100" />
              </Grid.ColumnDefinitions>

              <TextBlockGrid.Row="0" Grid.Column="0" Text="
                {Binding Name}" FontWeight="Bold"
                Foreground="OrangeRed"/>

              <TextBlockGrid.Row="0" Grid.Column="1"
                Text="{BindingDateDue}" />

              <TextBlockGrid.Row="0" Grid.Column="2"
                Text="{Binding Priority}" Foreground="Yellow"/>
```

```
            <TextBlockGrid.Row="1" Grid.ColumnSpan="3"
              Text="{Binding Notes}" />

            <TextBlockGrid.Row="2" Grid.ColumnSpan="3" />
          </Grid>
        </DataTemplate>
      </ListBox.ItemTemplate>
    </ListBox>
  </Grid>

  <Button Content="Save and Load Xml"
    Height="72" HorizontalAlignment="Left"
    Margin="24,48,0,0" Name="button1" VerticalAlignment="Top"
    Width="423" Grid.Row="1" Click="button1_Click" />

</Grid>
```

2. Add the `button1_Click` event method.

3. Press *F5* and the resulting page should look like the following screenshot:

4. Let's add a new class file and modify the `MyTask` class by adding serialization attributes as shown in the following code snippet. Here, `ElementName` indicates what name to use when creating the root XML element. The `XmlElement` attribute indicates each of the properties being used as attribute elements:

```
[XmlRootAttribute(ElementName="MyTask",IsNullable=false)]
public class MyTask
{
  [XmlElement]
  public string Name { get; set; }
  [XmlElement]
  public string Notes { get; set; }
  [XmlElement]
  public string Priority { get; set; }
  [XmlElement]
  publicDateTimeDateDue { get; set; }
  [XmlElement]
  publicDateTimeDateCreated { get; set; }
}
```

5. Add a reference to the assembly `System.Xml.Serialization` of the project and then add the `using` declaration to the `MainPage.xaml.cs` file.

6. Now add a method `SaveXmlToLocalStorage` to save the XML to local storage:

```
Private void SaveXmlToLocalStorage()
{

  List<MyTask>iTasks = new List<MyTask>
  {

    newMyTask(){Name = "Task Name 1",Notes = "Task Details 1",
      Priority = "High", DateDue = DateTime.Parse("7/01/2011"),
      DateCreated=DateTime.Now},

    newMyTask(){Name = "Task Name 2",Notes = "Task Details 2",
      Priority = "Low", DateDue = DateTime.Parse("10/01/2011"),
      DateCreated=DateTime.Now},

    newMyTask(){Name = "Task Name 3",Notes = "Task Details 3",
      Priority = "Medium", DateDue = DateTime.Parse("12/11/2011"),
      DateCreated=DateTime.Now}

  };

  XmlSerializerxmlSerializer=
    new XmlSerializer(typeof(List<MyTask>));
```

```
  using (IsolatedStorageFileisFile =
    IsolatedStorageFile.GetUserStoreForApplication())
  {
    using (IsolatedStorageFileStreamxmlStream =
    isFile.OpenFile(@"streamXmlFile.xml",
    System.IO.FileMode.OpenOrCreate))
    {
      xmlSerializer.Serialize(xmlStream, iTasks);
    }
  }
  xmlSerializer= null;
}
```

7. Add another method called `LoadXmlFromLocalStorage()` to deserialize the XML file from the local storage:

```
Private void LoadXmlFromLocalStorage()
{
  List<MyTask>iTasks = newList<MyTask>();

  XmlSerializerxmlSerializer=
    new XmlSerializer(typeof(List<MyTask>));

  using (IsolatedStorageFileisFile =
    IsolatedStorageFile.GetUserStoreForApplication())
  {

    if (isolatedStorage.FileExists(@"streamXmlFile.xml"))
    {
      using (StreamReader reader =
        new StreamReader(isolatedStorage.OpenFile
      (@"streamXmlFile.xml", FileMode.Open)))
      {
        iTasks = xmlSerializer.Deserialize(reader) asList<MyTask>;
      }
    }
  }

  lstTasks.ItemsSource = iTasks;

  xmlSerializer= null;
}
```

8. Now let's call the preceding two methods, `SaveXmlToLocalStorage()` and `LoadXmlFromLocalStorage()` in the button click event method:

```
private void button1_Click(object sender, RoutedEventArgs e)
{
  SaveXmlToLocalStorage();
  LoadXmlFromLocalStorage();
}
```

9. Press *F5* and click on the **Save and Load Xml** button. You should be able to serialize the sample XML to local storage and retrieve it back to display in the list box control. The result should look like the following screenshot:

How it works...

Initially we used the object initializer to create some test XML data as a list. Then we created the `XmlSerializer` object. Similar to recipes in *Chapter 2, Isolated Storage*, we opened the isolated storage `XMLstream` for creating the file and saving it. Then we used the `Serialize` method to write the XML document to a file called `streamXmlFile.xml` using the stream object.

Once the XML file is created in the local storage, we can use the same procedure as saving to open the file. While reading the XML file, we first check if the file exists in the isolated storage, then using the `StreamReader` object we open the file using the property `FileMode.Open`. We then deserialize the reader objects and convert them to a list collection.

There's more...

For more detailed information about the `XmlSerializer` class refer to the MSDN article at the following link:
`http://msdn.microsoft.com/en-us/library/system.xml.serialization.`
`xmlserializer.aspx`.

In the *Chapter 7, Windows Communication Framework*, we discuss how to consume **WCF (Windows Communication Foundation)** web services. In WCF, the default serializer used is `DataContractSerializer`. You can learn more on this topic at the following link:
`http://msdn.microsoft.com/en-us/library/ms731073.aspx`.

You can also serialize to **JSON (Java Script Object Notation)** using `DataContractJsonSerializer`. You can learn more about this class at the following link:
`http://msdn.microsoft.com/en-us/library/system.runtime.`
`serialization.json.datacontractjsonserializer(v=vs.95).aspx`.

Also, you can use the WCF attribute `ResponseFormat=WebMessageFormat.Xml` for XML format or `ResponseFormat=WebMessageFormat.Json` for JSON format.

See also

XML is not the only way to save information to local storage. Refer to *Chapter 5, Using On-Device Databases*, and you will learn how to save information using On-Device database options. Also, check *Chapter 7* to learn more on WCF.

4
Using Open Data

In this chapter, we will cover:

- ▸ Consuming OData services
- ▸ Searching OData services
- ▸ CRUD operations with OData

Introduction

Open Data is also known as **OData**. OData is a web protocol for querying and manipulating data. It uses the **REST** (**Representational State Transfer**) based URI syntax for querying and filtering data.

OData works over HTTP and follows a simple syntax, which can be used in accessing any web resource. Different operations such as create, read, update, and delete can be performed using a URI with query string syntax.

OData supports **AtomPub** (**Atom Publishing Protocol**) and **JSON** (**JavaScript Object Notation**) to access the data from different sources such as relational databases, file systems, content management systems, and websites. AtomPub is based on the W3 standard Atom (**RFC 4287**).

OData provides features built on top of AtomPub, which are for creating, updating, and deleting data. In addition to AtomPub features, OData also provides rich features for querying and manipulating data.

Windows Phone 7.1 SDK supports the following OData features:

- ▸ OData Client Library is included in the SDK, hence no separate download is required.
- ▸ You can now generate client proxy classes by adding the reference to the OData service feeds.

- ▸ Two main classes supported are `DataServiceContext` class and `DataServiceCollection<T>` class.

- ▸ LINQ queries to OData resources are supported. It continues to support URI-based queries as well.

- ▸ Client authentication is supported. Now you can use a username and password to authenticate the OData Service.

- ▸ It supports the ability to access binary data, for instance, to download a large media resource separate from the entity it belongs to.

- ▸ We can still use the `DataSvcUtil` to generate proxy classes with the command-line. Various arguments are available such as `/uri`, `/out`, `/in`, `/language`, `/version`, and `/DataServiceCollection`.

Consuming OData services

This recipe demonstrates how to access OData using a simple URI. For this recipe, we will use the `DataSvcUtil` to generate the proxy classes instead of adding a reference.

Getting ready

For this sample, we will be using an OData API exposed by Netflix, an online movie rental company. At the time of writing the book, this service was in preview mode; please refer to the online documentation for the latest changes:

1. Using your browser you can navigate to `http://developer.netflix.com/docs/oData_Catalog` to find all the documentation about the OData API.

2. You can browse OData using `http://odata.netflix.com/catalog/`. We will be using this link to consume the data in this recipe.

3. There are several features available for us to consume the data. At the resource level, we can get Catalog Titles (Catalog/Titles), People (Catalog/People), Languages (Catalog/Languages), and Genres (Catalog/Genres).

4. We can use `$filter` to get the lowest rated titles available to watch instantly or the highest rated titles.

5. Some of the parameters supported by Neflix are `filter`, `format`, `top/skip`, `orderby`, `expand`, `inlinecount`, and `select`.

6. Filter operators supported are `ge` (greater than or equal to), `gt` (greater than), `le` (less than or equal to), `lt` (less than), `eq` (equal to), and `ne` (not equal to).

7. Filter functions supported are `Date` (year, month, day, hour, minute, second), `String` (indexOf, replace, toLower, toUpper, trim, substring, concat, and length), and `Math` (Round, Ceiling, and Floor).

How to do it...

In this recipe we first generate the proxy class and then we add this file to the project. We then call the Netflix API to get the results, which are displayed in the listbox control.

1. Open a **New Project** and using the **Windows Phone Application** template create the project and name it `Recipe1_Netflix` under the solution folder `Ch4_Recipes`.

2. To consume the Netflix OData, we first need to generate the proxy class using the utility tool `DataSvcUtil`, which is a part of the Windows Phone 7.1 SDK. Use the following command line to generate the proxy class `NetflixModel`:

   ```
   datasvcutil /uri:http://odata.netflix.com/v1/Catalog/ /out:.\
   NetflixModel.cs /Version:2.0 /DataServiceCollection
   ```

```
C:\Windows\system32\cmd.exe                                    _  □  ⊠

Microsoft Windows [Version 6.1.7600]
Copyright (c) 2009 Microsoft Corporation.  All rights reserved.

C:\Users\user>cd \

C:\>cd DataSvc

C:\DataSvc>DataSvcUtil /uri:http://odata.netflix.com/v1/catalog /out:.\MyflixMod
el.cs /Version:2.0 /DataServiceCollection
Microsoft (R) DataSvcUtil version 1.0.0.0
Copyright (C) 2008 Microsoft Corporation. All rights reserved.

Writing object layer file...

Generation Complete -- 0 errors, 0 warnings

C:\DataSvc>
```

3. Now let's add the proxy file, `NetflixModel.cs`, which we generated into the project by right-clicking and choosing **Add Existing Item**. Alternatively, from Windows Explorer you can just copy and paste to the project.

4. Add a reference to the `System.Data.Services.Client` assembly, which comes with the SDK for the project.

5. Open the `MainPage.xaml` file, add a `TextBlock` control inside the `ListBox` and bind the control to `Name`. The title of the movie is the property Name returned from the Netflix Service.

```
<!--LayoutRoot is the root grid where all page content is
  placed-->
<Grid x:Name="LayoutRoot" Background="Transparent"
  DataContext="{Binding}">
  <Grid.RowDefinitions>
    <RowDefinition Height="Auto"/>
    <RowDefinition Height="*"/>
  </Grid.RowDefinitions>
```

```xml
<!--TitlePanel contains the name of the application and
    page title-->
<StackPanel x:Name="TitlePanel" Grid.Row="0"
   Margin="12,17,0,28">
     <TextBlock x:Name="ApplicationTitle" Text=
       "Ch4 Recipes" Style="{StaticResource
       PhoneTextNormalStyle}"/>
     <TextBlock x:Name="PageTitle" Text="Movie Titles"
       Margin="9,-7,0,0" Style="{StaticResource
       PhoneTextTitle1Style}"/>
</StackPanel>

<!--ContentPanel - place additional content here-->
<Grid x:Name="ContentPanel" Margin="12,0,12,-13" Grid.Row="1">
   <ListBox x:Name ="lstTasks" Grid.Row="3" Grid.Column ="1">
     <ListBox.ItemTemplate>
       <DataTemplate>
         <Grid>
           <Grid.RowDefinitions>
             <RowDefinition Height="*" />
             <RowDefinition Height="*" />
           </Grid.RowDefinitions>

           <Grid.ColumnDefinitions>
             <ColumnDefinition Width="*" />
           </Grid.ColumnDefinitions>

           <TextBlock Grid.Row="0" TextWrapping="Wrap"
             Text="{Binding Name}" FontWeight="Bold"
             FontStretch="Expanded" Foreground="OrangeRed"/>
         </Grid>
       </DataTemplate>
     </ListBox.ItemTemplate>
   </ListBox>
  </Grid>
</Grid>
```

6. Open the `MainPage.xaml.cs` file and include the following two references:

```csharp
using NetflixCatalog.Model;
using System.Data.Services.Client;
```

7. Let's add the loaded event to the page from the `MainPage.xaml` file and click on `<New Eventhandler>`. Give it the name `MainPage_Loaded`. Check the last line in the following code:

```
<phone:PhoneApplicationPage
  x:Class="Recipe1_Netflix.MainPage"
  xmlns="http://schemas.microsoft.com/winfx/2006/
    xaml/presentation"
  xmlns:x="http://schemas.microsoft.com/winfx/2006/xaml"
  xmlns:phone="clr-namespace:Microsoft.Phone.Controls;
    assembly=Microsoft.Phone"
  xmlns:shell="clr-namespace:Microsoft.Phone.Shell;
    assembly=Microsoft.Phone"
  xmlns:d="http://schemas.microsoft.com/expression/blend/2008"
  xmlns:mc="http://schemas.openxmlformats.org/
    markup-compatibility/2006"
  mc:Ignorable="d" d:DesignWidth="480" d:DesignHeight="768"
  FontFamily="{StaticResource PhoneFontFamilyNormal}"
  FontSize="{StaticResource PhoneFontSizeNormal}"
  Foreground="{StaticResource PhoneForegroundBrush}"
  SupportedOrientations="Portrait" Orientation="Portrait"
  shell:SystemTray.IsVisible="True" Loaded="MainPage_Loaded">
```

8. Now right-click on **MainPage_Loaded** and select **Navigate to Event Handler**. This creates the method `MainPage_Loaded`.

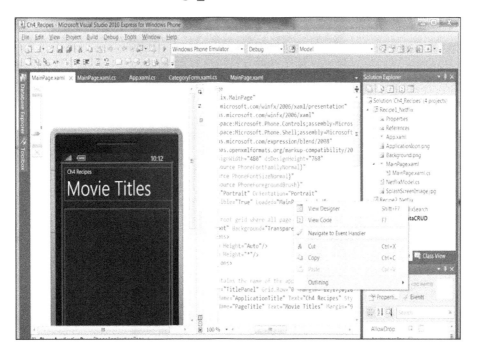

9. In the `MainPage_Loaded` method, we will add the code to navigate to the service URI. Here we create an instance of `Uri` with the Netflix service URI. Then, we will use the generic `DataServiceCollection` to get the Titles from the model. Then we will call the `LoadAsync` method with the query `"Titles"`:

```
public MainPage_Loaded(object sender,RoutedEventArgs e)
{
  Uri svcUri = new Uri(@"http://odata.netflix.com/v1/Catalog/");
  var query = "Titles";
  // create context
  NetflixCatalog.Model.NetflixCatalog ctx = new
    NetflixCatalog.Model.NetflixCatalog(svcUri);

  DataServiceCollection<NetflixCatalog.Model.Title> rslts = new
    DataServiceCollection<NetflixCatalog.Model.Title>(ctx);

  rslts.LoadAsync(new Uri(query,UriKind.Relative));

  lstTasks.ItemsSource = rslts;
}
```

10. Press *F5* to run. If there are no errors, then you should see all the movies in a list:

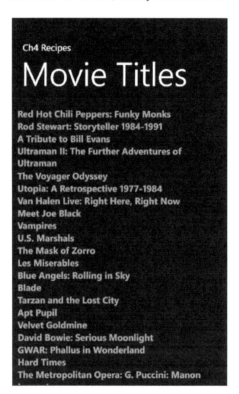

How it works...

In the first step, we created a `Uri` object with the OData provider URI. We used two arguments, `/Version` and `/DataServiceCollection`. The version is 2.0, which is the latest. `DataServiceCollection` supports a read/write model that tracks changes automatically. In the `MainPage_Loaded` event method, we created instances of the `DataServiceCollection` and the `Context` objects. Then, we sent the request using the `LoadAsync` method by passing the query string `Titles`. Finally, we loaded the results to the `ListBox`.

There's more...

The Netflix API reference provides us with many different options to consume the data for customizing the client. You can add more features to your own app or to one of the recipes discussed in this chapter.

Using Reference to create the proxy class

In the last recipe, we learned how to consume the OData service by generating proxy classes using `DataSvcUtil`. Now with Phone 7.1 SDK, adding the reference to the project creates the proxy classes automatically. Let's repeat the same sample in the following steps:

1. Add a new project by right-clicking the preceding solution, `Ch4_Recipes`, and create a new Phone 7 project and name it `Recipe1_MyFlicks1`. Pick the SDK version 7.1 in the dialog box.

2. Right-click the project in the solution explorer and select **Add Service Reference...**. In the dialog box type the address `http://odata.netflix.com/Catalog/` and click on **Go**. You should see the list of available service APIs in the Netflix Catalog. Change the default service reference name to `NetflixReference`. All the available entities exposed by the Netflix service are displayed in the left listbox. This is shown in the following screenshot:

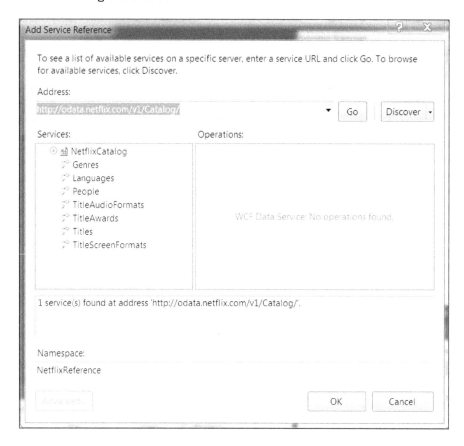

3. After you complete adding the reference, you should see both `References` and `Service References` folders updated as shown in the following screenshot:

4. Now open the `MainPage.xaml` file and copy the XAML shown in the following code snippet, which will add a listbox control with a text block control:

```xml
<!--LayoutRoot is the root grid where all page content is
  placed-->
<Grid x:Name="LayoutRoot" Background="Transparent"
  DataContext="{Binding}">
  <Grid.RowDefinitions>
    <RowDefinition Height="Auto"/>
    <RowDefinition Height="*"/>
  </Grid.RowDefinitions>

  <!--TitlePanel contains the name of the application and
    page title-->
  <StackPanel x:Name="TitlePanel" Grid.Row="0"
    Margin="12,17,0,28">
      <TextBlock x:Name="ApplicationTitle" Text=
        "Ch4 Recipes" Style="{StaticResource
        PhoneTextNormalStyle}"/>
```

```xml
        <TextBlock x:Name="PageTitle" Text="Movie Titles"
          Margin="9,-7,0,0" Style="{StaticResource
          PhoneTextTitle1Style}"/>
    </StackPanel>

    <!--ContentPanel - place additional content here-->
    <Grid x:Name="ContentPanel" Margin="12,0,12,-13" Grid.Row="1">
      <ListBox x:Name ="lstTasks" Grid.Row="3" Grid.Column ="1">
        <ListBox.ItemTemplate>
          <DataTemplate>
            <Grid>
              <Grid.RowDefinitions>
                <RowDefinition Height="*" />
                <RowDefinition Height="*" />
              </Grid.RowDefinitions>

              <Grid.ColumnDefinitions>
                <ColumnDefinition Width="*" />
              </Grid.ColumnDefinitions>

              <TextBlock Grid.Row="0" TextWrapping="Wrap"
                Text="{Binding Name}" FontWeight="Bold"
                FontStretch="Expanded" Foreground="OrangeRed"/>
            </Grid>
          </DataTemplate>
        </ListBox.ItemTemplate>
      </ListBox>
    </Grid>
  </Grid>
```

5. Open the `MainPage.xaml.cs` file and add `using` references at the top of the page to the `System.Data.Services.Client` and `Recipe2_Netflix. NetflixReferece`:

```csharp
using System.Data.Services.Client;
using Recipe2_Netflix.NetflixReference;
```

6. In the `MainPage.xaml` file, add the loaded event by right-clicking the `<New EventHandler>`. Navigate to the event handler `PhoneApplicationPage_ Loaded`.

```csharp
private void PhoneApplicationPage_Loaded(object sender,
  RoutedEventArgs e)
{

}
```

7. Now, let's add the code to the preceding loaded event. Here we create an instance of `NetflixCatalog` using the service `Uri`. Then, using the `DataServiceCollection`, we get the genre as a list and call the `LoadCompleted` event. Using LINQ to Objects, we query all the genres and pass the query to the `LoadAsync` method.

```
private void PhoneApplicationPage_Loaded(object sender,
  RoutedEventArgs e)
{
  Uri svcUri = new Uri(@"http://odata.netflix.com/Catalog/");
  ctx= new NetflixCatalog(svcUri);
  lstGenres = new DataServiceCollection<Genre>();
  lstGenres.LoadCompleted += new EventHandler
    <LoadCompletedEventArgs>(lstGenres_LoadCompleted);

  var query = from g in ctx.Genres select g;
  lstGenres.LoadAsync(query);
}
```

8. Next, we add the new event method, `lstGenres_LoadCompleted`. In this method, we assign the genre list `lstGenres` to `lstBoxItems.ItemsSource`:

```
void lstGenres_LoadCompleted(object sender,
  LoadCompletedEventArgs e)
{
  if (lstGenres.Continuation != null)
  {
    lstGenres.LoadNextPartialSetAsync();
  }
  else
  {
    this.lstBoxItems.ItemsSource = lstGenres;
  }
}
```

9. Press *F5*. You should see the list of all genres available in the Netflix database:

See also

Check the next recipe for more on how to search the Netflix catalog. Also, check the following online resources to understand more on OData support in Phone 7.1 SDK:

`http://msdn.microsoft.com/en-us/library/gg521146(v=vs.92).aspx.`

Searching OData services

In this recipe let's search OData using `$filter`. Netflix OData API supports `$filter`.

Getting ready

Let's create a new solution and name it `Recipe3_NetflixSearch` or copy the project from `Recipe1_Netflix` under the folder `Ch4_Recipes`.

How to do it...

1. Open `MainPage.xaml` and add a text block, textbox, and a search button:

```
<Grid x:Name="LayoutRoot" Background="Transparent"
  DataContext="{Binding}">
  <Grid.RowDefinitions>
    <RowDefinition Height="152"/>
    <RowDefinition Height="234"/>
    <RowDefinition Height="382*"/>
  </Grid.RowDefinitions>

  <!--TitlePanel contains the name of the application and page
    title-->

  <StackPanel x:Name="TitlePanel" Grid.Row="0"
    Margin="12,17,0,28">

    <TextBlock x:Name="ApplicationTitle" Text="Ch4 Recipes"
      Style="{StaticResource PhoneTextNormalStyle}"/>
    <TextBlock x:Name="PageTitle" Text="Netflix Search" Margin="9,
      -7,0,0" Style="{StaticResource PhoneTextTitle1Style}"/>

  </StackPanel>

  <StackPanel x:Name="SearchPanel" Grid.Row="1" Margin="0,0,0,31">
    <TextBlock Height="41" Margin="6,6,0,0" Name="textBlock1"
      Text="Search for the Movie Titles:" Width="460" />
    <TextBox Height="77" Margin="0,0,0,0" Name="txtSearch" Text=""
      Width="483" />
    <Button Content="Search" Height="77" Margin="0,0,0,0"
      Name="btnSearch" Width="160" Click="btnSearch_Click" />

  </StackPanel>

  <!--ContentPanel - place additional content here-->
  <Grid x:Name="ContentPanel" Margin="12,222,12,0" Grid.Row="1"
    Grid.RowSpan="2">
    <Grid.ColumnDefinitions>
      <ColumnDefinition Width="223*" />
      <ColumnDefinition Width="4*" />
```

```
            <ColumnDefinition Width="229" />
        </Grid.ColumnDefinitions>
        <ListBox x:Name ="lstResult" Grid.ColumnSpan="3"
          Margin="0,0,0,6" ItemsSource="{Binding}">

            <ListBox.ItemTemplate>
              <DataTemplate>
                <Grid>
                  <Grid.RowDefinitions>
                    <RowDefinition Height="*" />
                    <RowDefinition Height="*" />
                  </Grid.RowDefinitions>

                  <Grid.ColumnDefinitions>
                    <ColumnDefinition Width="*" />
                  </Grid.ColumnDefinitions>

                  <TextBlock TextWrapping="Wrap" Text="{Binding
                    Path=Name}" FontWeight="Bold" FontStretch="Expanded"
                    Foreground="OrangeRed"/>
                </Grid>
              </DataTemplate>
            </ListBox.ItemTemplate>
        </ListBox>
      </Grid>
  </Grid>
```

2. Open the `MainPage.xaml.cs` file and add the following three private variables:

```
private Uri svcUri;
private NetflixCatalog.Model.NetflixCatalog ctx;
private DataServiceCollection<NetflixCatalog.Model.Title> rslts;
```

3. Next, in the `MainPage_Loaded` method, initialize the `Uri` to the OData service. Then, we will instantiate the context object using the `NetflixCatalog` method by passing the service `Uri`. Use the `DataServiceCollection` to store the title list. Add the event handler for the `rslts_LoadCompleted` method. Finally, run the query using the `LoadAsync` method:

```
public MainPage_Loaded(object sender,RoutedEventArgs e)
{
  InitializeComponent();

  svcUri = new Uri(@"http://odata.netflix.com/v1/Catalog/");
  // create context
  ctx = new NetflixCatalog.Model.NetflixCatalog(svcUri);
```

```
rslts = new DataServiceCollection
  <NetflixCatalog.Model.Title>(ctx);
rslts.LoadCompleted += new EventHandler
  <LoadCompletedEventArgs> (rslts_LoadCompleted);

var query = "Titles";
rslts.Clear();
rslts.LoadAsync(new Uri(query, UriKind.Relative));
}
```

4. Let's add the event handler method. Here, we check for any error. If there is any error found, then we display a message; otherwise we load the results into `ListBox`. Here you can notice, we didn't refer to the `ListBox` control; `DataContext` automatically takes care of that:

```
private void rslts_LoadCompleted(object sender,
  LoadCompletedEventArgs e)
{
  if (e.Error == null)
  {
    this.DataContext = rslts;
  }
  else
  {
    MessageBox.Show(string.Format("Error: {0}", e.Error.Message));
  }
}
```

5. Finally, let's add the button event method for the `Search` button click event:

```
private void btnSearch_Click(object sender, RoutedEventArgs e)
{
  var qry = String.Format("/Titles?$filter=substringof
    ('{0}',Name)", txtSearch.Text);
  rslts.Clear();
  rslts.LoadAsync(new Uri(qry, UriKind.Relative));
}
```

6. Press *F5* to run. Type in a random movie title, for example '**avatar**', and click on the **Search** button. If the movie exists in the database, then it will display all the titles containing the search string as shown in the following screenshot:

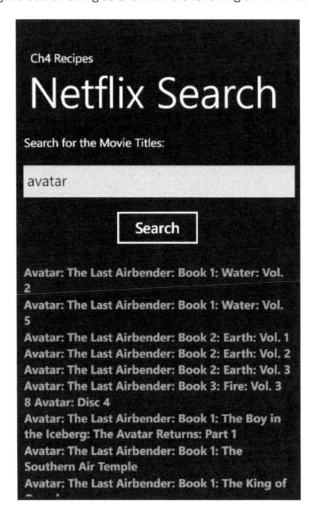

How it works...

We declared a `Context` class for `NetflixCatalog` and `DataServiceCollection` before the `MainPage` method.

We hooked up an `EventHandler` to the `LoadCompleted` event. Here we check for errors while loading the results. If there are no errors, then we load the results to the data context object.

Next, we added a click event method for the `Search` button where we take the search string from the search textbox and build the query string using the `$filter` parameter. Then, we query `DataServiceCollection` again.

There's more...

Netflix supports many other parameters that can be used for various filters and search options.

Different parameters supported by Netflix OData

1. **Format**: You can format the result using a format parameter, either JSON or Atom.

2. **Top/skip**: This can be used for paging options with values as integer.

3. **Orderby**: You can sort the results with `orderby` in the resource field.

4. **Expand**: This is used for expanding the fields inline using the resource fields.

5. **Inlinecount**: This can be used for getting the overall count using values such as `allpages`.

6. **Select**: This is used for selecting the fields to return.

See also

In the next recipe, we will learn how to edit, update and delete the OData.

CRUD operations with OData

In this recipe we will discuss how to implement create, update, and delete operations, also known as CRUD operations using `DataServiceCollection` and `Context` class. Here are the mappings for HTTP Verb to OData operation:

HTTP	OData
GET	Read
POST	Update
PUT	Insert
DELETE	Delete

Getting ready

For this sample, we will be using the editable OData API exposed by `odata.org`. Just a note, at the time of writing the book this service was provided for testing OData edit features with some restrictions.

You can browse OData using `http://services.odata.org/ (S(bltvbobia1rthiavqczdcr1u))/OData/OData.svc/`. We will be using this link to consume the data in this recipe. For simplicity, we shall only update the categories.

How to do it...

To consume sample editable OData, we first need to generate the proxy class using the `DataSvcUtil` using the following command-line:

```
datasvcutil /uri:http://services.odata.org/(S(bltvbobia1rthiavqczdcr1u))/
OData/OData.svc/ /out:.\EditODataModel.cs /Version:2.0 /
DataServiceCollection
```

1. Right-click on the solution folder `Ch4_Recipes` and add a new Phone Project with a name `Recipe4_ODataCRUD`.

2. Now add the proxy class `EditODataModel.cs` we generated into the project by right-clicking and selecting **Add Existing Item**. You can also use Windows Explorer to just copy and paste the file into the project.

3. Add a reference to the assembly `System.Data.Services.Client` that comes with the SDK to the project.

4. Open the `MainPage.xaml` file and let's add a `ListBox` control with two text blocks, one for Category ID and another for Category Name. Add the `Binding` property to both of them. Also, add the `SelectionChanged` event for the `ListBox`. Right-click on **OnSelect** and click on **Navigate to Event Handler** to create the empty `OnSelect` event method:

```xml
<Grid x:Name="LayoutRoot" Background="Transparent">
  <Grid.RowDefinitions>
    <RowDefinition Height="Auto"/>
    <RowDefinition Height="*"/>
  </Grid.RowDefinitions>

  <!--TitlePanel contains the name of the application and page
    title-->
  <StackPanel x:Name="TitlePanel" Grid.Row="0"
    Margin="12,17,0,28">
    <TextBlock x:Name="ApplicationTitle" Text="Ch4 Recipes"
      Style="{StaticResource PhoneTextNormalStyle}"/>

    <TextBlock x:Name="PageTitle" Text="OData CRUD" Margin="9,-
      7,0,0" Style="{StaticResource PhoneTextTitle1Style}"/>
  </StackPanel>

  <!--ContentPanel - place additional content here-->
  <Grid x:Name="ContentPanel" Grid.Row="1" Margin="12,0,12,0">
    <ListBox x:Name ="lstResults" Grid.Row="3" Grid.Column ="1"
      ItemsSource="{Binding}" SelectionChanged="OnSelect">
      <ListBox.ItemTemplate>
        <DataTemplate>
          <Grid>
            <Grid.RowDefinitions>
              <RowDefinition Height="*" />
              <RowDefinition Height="*" />
            </Grid.RowDefinitions>

            <Grid.ColumnDefinitions>
              <ColumnDefinition Width="20"/>
              <ColumnDefinition Width="*" />
            </Grid.ColumnDefinitions>

            <TextBlock Grid.Row="0" Grid.Column="0" Text="{Binding
              ID}" FontWeight="Bold" Foreground="OrangeRed"/>
            <TextBlock Grid.Row="0" Grid.Column="1"
              TextWrapping="Wrap" Text="{Binding Name}"
              FontWeight="Bold" FontStretch="Expanded"
              Foreground="OrangeRed"/>
```

```
            </Grid>
          </DataTemplate>
        </ListBox.ItemTemplate>
      </ListBox>

    </Grid>
  </Grid>
```

5. Windows Phone 7.1 SDK comes with most commonly used icons. Create a new folder in the project and name it `Images`. Now right-click on the `Images` folder and select **Add Existing Items**. Navigate to your local drive `Program Files\Microsoft SDKs\` as shown in the following screenshot and select `appbar.new.rest.png`.

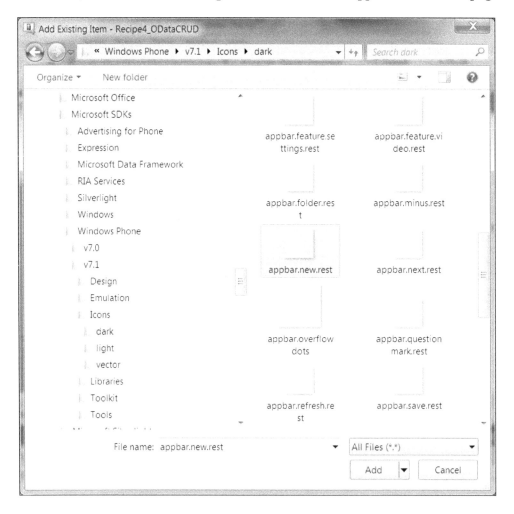

6. After the grid, add the `ApplicationBar` at the bottom to display one icon to add a new `Category`. Also, add the click event to map to the `ButtonAdd_Click` method:

```
<phone:PhoneApplicationPage.ApplicationBar>
  <shell:ApplicationBar BackgroundColor="Orange" IsVisible="True"
    IsMenuEnabled="True">
    <shell:ApplicationBarIconButton
      IconUri="/Images/appbar.new.rest.png"
      Click="ButtonAdd_Click" Text="Add Task"/>
  </shell:ApplicationBar>
</phone:PhoneApplicationPage.ApplicationBar>
```

7. Open the `MainPage.xaml.cs` file and include the following `using` declarations at the beginning of the page:

```
using ODataDemo;
using System.Data.Services.Client;
using System.Windows.Controls.Primitives;
```

8. Let's add the following variables just before the `MainPage` constructor:

```
private Uri svcUri;
private ODataDemo.DemoService ctx;
private DataServiceCollection<ODataDemo.Category> rslts;
```

9. Next, add the following code to the `MainPage` method. Here we are creating the instance of the `Uri` and calling the `DemoService`. Similar to the last recipe, we will save the `Category` collections in the `DataServiceCollection` and call `LoadAsync`:

```
public MainPage_Loaded(object sender, RoutedEventArgs e)
{
  svcUri = new Uri(@"http://services.odata.org/
    (S(bltvbobia1rthiavqczdcr1u))/OData/OData.svc/");
  var query = "Categories";
  // create context
  ctx = new ODataDemo.DemoService(svcUri);

  rslts = new DataServiceCollection<ODataDemo.Category>(ctx);
  rslts.LoadCompleted += new EventHandler
    <LoadCompletedEventArgs>(rslts_LoadCompleted);

  rslts.LoadAsync(new Uri(query, UriKind.Relative));

}
```

10. Let's add the method `rslts_LoadCompleted`. Here we check for any errors, otherwise we assign the query results to the `DataContext`:

```
private void rslts_LoadCompleted(object sender,
  LoadCompletedEventArgs e)
{
  if (e.Error == null)
  {
    this.DataContext = rslts;
  }
  else
  {
  MessageBox.Show(string.Format("Error: {0}", e.Error.Message));
  }
}
```

11. Now let's add the code in the `OnSelect` event method. Here we get the `SelectedIndex` and pass it as a query string. This is used for selecting:

```
private void OnSelect(object sender, SelectionChangedEventArgs e)
{
  var selector = (Selector)sender;
  if (selector.SelectedIndex == -1)
    return;

  this.NavigationService.Navigate(new
    Uri("/CategoryForm.xaml?selIndex = "
    + selector.SelectedIndex, UriKind.Relative));

  selector.SelectedIndex = -1;
}
```

12. Next, we added the toolbar at the bottom for adding new items. Let's add the method to navigate to `CategoryForm.xaml` with query string `selIndex` as zero. The reason for zero is to indicate that it is a new category:

```
private void ButtonAdd_Click(object sender, EventArgs e)
{
  this.NavigationService.Navigate(new
    Uri("/CategoryForm.xaml?selIndex = 0", UriKind.Relative));
}
```

13. Now let's add a new page called `CategoryForm.xaml` to the project. As this is for updating the `Category` collection, let's add two textboxes and a save button, which would look like the following code snippet:

```
<Grid x:Name="LayoutRoot" Background="Transparent">
  <Grid.RowDefinitions>
    <RowDefinition Height="Auto"/>
```

```
                  <RowDefinition Height="*"/>
                </Grid.RowDefinitions>

                <!--TitlePanel contains the name of the application and page
                  title-->
                <StackPanel x:Name="TitlePanel" Grid.Row="0"
                  Margin="12,17,0,28">
                <TextBlock x:Name="ApplicationTitle" Text="Edit OData App"
                  Style="{StaticResource PhoneTextNormalStyle}"/>
                <TextBlock x:Name="PageTitle" Text="Category" Margin="9,-7,0,0"
                  Style="{StaticResource PhoneTextTitle1Style}"/>
                </StackPanel>

                <!--ContentPanel - place additional content here-->
                <Grid x:Name="ContentPanel" Grid.Row="1" Margin="12,0,12,0">
                  <TextBlock Height="30" HorizontalAlignment="Left"
                    Margin="28,43,0,0" Name="textBlock1" Text="ID"
                    VerticalAlignment="Top" Width="115" />
                  <TextBox Height="72" HorizontalAlignment="Left"
                    Margin="12,68,0,0" Name="txtID" Text=""
                    VerticalAlignment="Top" Width="438" />
                  <TextBlock Height="30" HorizontalAlignment="Left"
                    Margin="28,146,0,0" Name="textBlock2" Text="Name"
                    VerticalAlignment="Top" Width="115" />
                  <TextBox Height="72" HorizontalAlignment="Left"
                    Margin="12,171,0,0" Name="txtName" Text=""
                    VerticalAlignment="Top" Width="438" />
                  <Button Content="Save" Height="72" HorizontalAlignment="Left"
                    Margin="12,249,0,0" Name="button2" VerticalAlignment="Top"
                    Width="136" />
                </Grid>
              </Grid>
```

14. Now, open the `CategoryForm.xaml.cs` file and add a `using` declaration at the top of the page for `ODataDemo`:

    ```
    using ODataDemo;
    ```

15. Next, we need to hold the new form data and when the **Save** button is clicked it should be accessed in the `MainPage` so it is added to the `DataServiceCollection`. We can achieve this by either serializing the object to local storage, or just holding a global static variable. Open the `App.xaml.cs` file and add static variable `_category`:

    ```
    public static OData Demo.Category _category;
    ```

16. When the user clicks the **Save** button, we save the ID and Name to the global variable and then navigate back to the previous page:

```
private void btnSave_Click(object sender, RoutedEventArgs e)
{
  App._category = new Category();
  if (txtID.Text != "")
    App._category.ID = int.Parse(txtID.Text);

  if (txtName.Text != "")
    App._category.Name = txtName.Text;

  NavigationService.GoBack();
}
```

17. Now open the MainPage.xaml.cs file and add the OnNavigatedTo method. In this method, we check if there is anything in the static variable and then add the category object to the collection.

```
// called when the current frame becomes active
protected override void OnNavigatedTo(System.Windows.Navigation.
  NavigationEventArgs e)
{
  if (App._category != null)
  {
    rslts.Add(App._category);
  }

  base.OnNavigatedTo(e);
}
```

18. Let's go back to CategoryForm.xaml.cs and add the OnNavigatedTo method here too. Before the method, declare the string variable selIndex. We will get the query string selIndex using the NavigationContext class. We will use this variable in the page-loaded event method to get the collection item.

```
private string selIndex;

protected override void OnNavigatedTo
  (System.Windows.Navigation.NavigationEventArgs e)
{
  base.OnNavigatedTo(e);
  if (!NavigationContext.QueryString.TryGetValue("selIndex", out
    selIndex))
  {
    MessageBox.Show("Error");
  }
```

```
}

private void PhoneApplicationPage_Loaded(object sender,
  RoutedEventArgs e)
{
  if (int.Parse(selIndex) != 0)
  {
    txtID.Text = App._category.ID.ToString();
    txtName.Text = App._category.Name.ToString();
  }
}
```

19. Now, press *F5* and run. You should see the list of categories and when you select the category name you will be navigated to `CategoryForm` to edit and save. You can also click on the **+** button in the navigation bar to save a new category.

How it works...

First, we displayed the list of categories available in the OData list. By getting the list using `DataServiceCollection` and context classes, we are making use of the automatic tracking for changes to the list.

By updating the object it is marked as changed. OData automatically updates the OData data source. We can add to and update the collection using `DataServiceCollection`'s add and update methods. Just like adding to and updating the collection, we can also remove from the collection.

There's more...

You can easily navigate the structure of OData using free tools available online.

OData Explorer

There are many different explorers available online for browsing the OData:

1. OData Explorer by Microsoft:

    `http://www.silverlight.net/content/samples/odataexplorer/default.html`

2. SESAME Data Browser also supports OData. At the time of writing this book, this was still a BETA:

    `http://metasapiens.com/sesame/data-browser/preview/`

3. LINQPad is another choice that supports OData:

    `http://www.linqpad.net/`

See also

Check *Chapter 6* for REST web services and *Chapter 7* for WCF web services.

Also, check the following online resources for further understanding of OData:

*   Consuming OData with MVVM for Windows Phone:

    `http://msdn.microsoft.com/en-us/library/hh394007(v=VS.92).aspx`

*   Building great experiences on any device with OData:

    `http://msdn.microsoft.com/en-us/magazine/hh394150.aspx`

*   Updating OData data sources from WP7 9 (OData Azure Service).

    `http://samidipbasu.com/2011/07/24/updating-odata-data-source-from-wp7-part-1/`

5
Using On-Device Databases

In this chapter, we will:

- ▸ Get an overview of SQLite Studio
- ▸ Explore creating and editing an SQLite file
- ▸ Learn how to use SQLite as an embedded database
- ▸ Get an overview of Microsoft SQL CE
- ▸ Learn how to create and delete data in SQL CE using LINQ to SQL
- ▸ Cover McObject's Perst as an embedded object data store
- ▸ Learn to save and delete data in the Perst database

Introduction

In *Chapter 3*, *XML as a Data Store*, we learned how we can persist data to local storage using Object serialization and XML. In this chapter, we shall discuss different options available for both commercial and open source on-device databases.

- ▸ **SQLite Client for Phone 7**: This is ported from the popular SQLite to work on Phone 7 devices
- ▸ **Microsoft SQL CE**: This is the Microsoft SQL Server Compact Edition
- ▸ **McObject's Perst**: This is a commercial On-Device database

Overview of SQLite Studio

In this recipe, we shall learn how to use the **SQLite Studio** for creating, editing, and querying an embedded SQLite database file.

Getting ready

First, let's download SQLite Studio, a free tool available online at `http://sqlitestudio.one.pl/`. SQLite Studio has a simple graphical user interface that helps in creating, inserting, and updating tables. Save the SQLite Studio `.exe` file to your local drive and then launch it.

How to do it...

In this recipe, we are going to create a database using SQLite Studio, and then create a table and add different columns. Once the table schema is created, we then add a couple of test records using the insert query statements.

1. Launch SQLite Studio and navigate to **Databases | Add Database**. Pick the folder you want to create this database in and select the option **Type name in field below:** and then type **MyDatabase**. You can also pick the version of SQLite you want to create. Click on **OK** to create and add the database file.

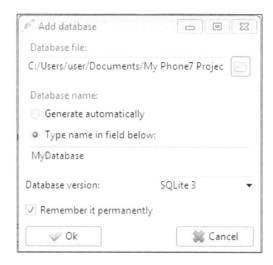

2. Once you open the database you have to right-click and connect it to open it.

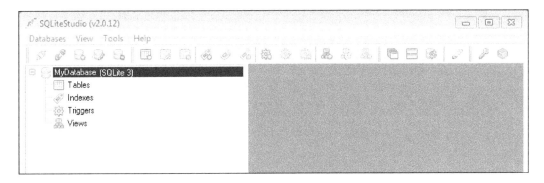

3. Add a table called `MyTasks` and add Primary Key column **Id**. Select the constraints **Primary Key**, **Unique**, and **Not NULL** checkboxes as shown in the following screenshot:

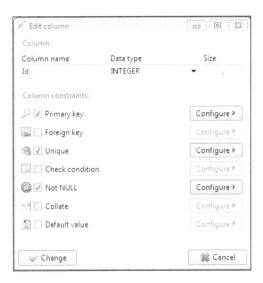

4. Repeat the steps to add all the columns so it looks like the following screenshot:

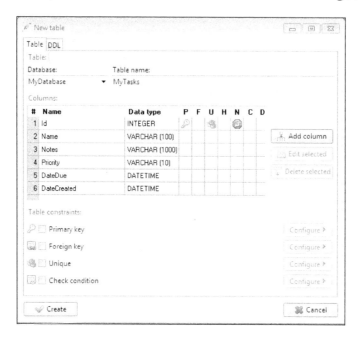

5. Once the table is created, we can now add two rows of test data using the following insert statements. Open the **SQL query** window and copy the `insert` statements as shown in the following code snippet:

```
insert into MyTasks values (1,'Task Name 1', 'Task Note 1',
'High','9/1/2011',date('now'));


insert into MyTasks values (2,'Task Name 2', 'Task Note 2',
'High','9/1/2011',date('now'));
```

6. Run the `select` query to return all the rows from the table `MyTasks`:

```
Select * from MyTasks
```

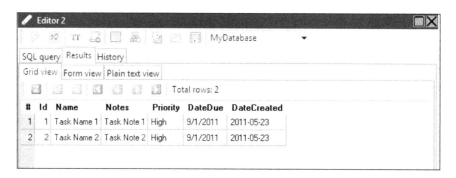

How it works...

We first created a local database file called `MyDatabase`. This file has an extension `.sqlite`. Then we created the `MyTasks` table with all the columns we needed for our `MyTasks` app. This is like creating tables in **SQL Server Management Studio**. Finally, we used simple SQL scripts to insert and query the test data.

There's more...

In this recipe, we learned how to create a SQLite file with tables and data. In the next couple of recipes, we shall explore how to use this file as a local database.

See also

Check the following recipe for how to access the SQLite file.

SQLite Client as an embedded database

In this recipe, we will explore how to use the SQLite Client CodePlex—an open source database **API (application programming interface)**—to open, save, delete, update, and close the SQLite file.

Getting ready

Download SQLite Client from the following address: `http://sqlitewindowsphone.codeplex.com/releases`. At the time of writing this book, the latest stable version was Rel 2. Ver 0.6.1. Download the zipped file and unzip it to a local folder.

Documents library	Arrange by:	Folder ▼
SQLLite		
Name	Date modified	Type
Community.CsharpSqlite.WP	12/27/2010 12:22 PM	File folder
CSharpSqlite.TestProject	11/30/2010 11:37 AM	File folder
MyTasks	4/7/2011 12:46 PM	File folder
WP7SQLiteClient	5/22/2011 11:13 PM	File folder
Community.CsharpSqlite.WP	7/20/2010 2:40 PM	Microsoft Visual Studio Solution
WP7SQLiteClient	2/25/2011 9:14 AM	Microsoft Visual Studio Solution

How to do it...

In this recipe, we will explore the test sample that comes with the SQLite Client SDK download. This sample demonstrates pretty much all the different features of SQLite embedded database.

1. Open the `Community.CsharpSqlite.WP` solution.

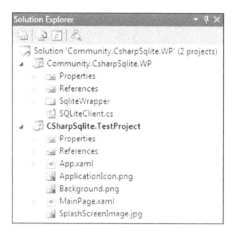

2. Press *F5* to see the results as shown in the following screenshot. The main page has different buttons to showcase SQLite's capabilities. This test application can be used to open and close the database. Once the database is open, we can create as well as drop the table using the **Create Table** and **Drop Table** buttons, respectively. You can use the **Generate Data** button to generate some random data, which you can see as results. Finally, you can delete the data you generated in the database.

How it works...

The `Community.CsharpSqlite.WP` project basically has `SqliteWrapper` classes for the entire SQLite software library. The `SQLiteClient.cs` file has different functions such as `ExecuteNonQuery`, `ExecuteQuery`, `ExecuteScalar`, `SQLiteCommand`, and so on. `SQLiteConnection` is used to open the database and the `Dispose()` method is called to close the database file.

`CreateCommand` and `ExecuteNonQuery` are used for creating the table along with simple SQL statements such as `Create table <table name>` and `Drop table <table name>`. We used insert query `insert into <table name> () values ()` to insert the data and then we used the delete query `delete <table name> where <conditional statement>` to delete the records in the table.

There's more...

In this recipe, we learned different aspects of operating and maintaining SQLite database files. SQLite is a powerful solution for saving the data locally and for using simple SQL queries. You can learn more about this by studying the samples included in the download folder `WP7SQLiteClient`.

See also

In the next recipe we shall learn how we can use SQLite in our `MyTasks` app. Also, check the recipe *SQL CE as a local store* as an alternative solution.

Using SQLite as a local store for the MyTasks App

In this recipe let's explore how to use the SQLite file we created in the first recipe, *Overview of SQLite Studio*, as the local data store for our `MyTasks` app.

Getting ready

For this recipe we shall use the project template we created in the *Chapter 1, Data Binding to UI Elements*.

How to do it...

In the following steps, we will create a `MyTasks` project to use the sample SQLite database file we created in the preceding recipe and then learn how to use the SQLite Client API to insert and display the results.

1. Create a project from the `CH1_MyTasks` template and name it `Ch5_MyTasks_SQLiteClient`.

2. Add the existing file `MyDatabase.sqlite` we created in the first recipe, *Overview of SQLite Studio*, and add it to the project root folder.

3. Copy the `DBHelper.cs` file from the SQLite Client project in the new folder `Helpers`.

4. Add a project reference to the assembly `Community.CsharpSqlite.WP.dll`.

5. Open the `App.xaml.cs` file and add `using` declaratives at the top of the file:

   ```
   using Ch5_MyTasks_SQLiteClient.Helpers;
   using System.Reflection;
   ```

6. Next in the `App` class, declare the following `get` property:

   ```
   private DBHelper _db;
   public DBHelper db
   {
     get
     {
       Assembly assem = Assembly.GetExecutingAssembly();

       if (_db == null)
       _db = new DBHelper(assem.FullName.Substring(0,
         assem.FullName.IndexOf(',')), "MyDatabase.sqlite");
       return _db;
     }
   }
   ```

7. Now open `MainPage.xaml` and add the declaration for `myTasks` collections:

   ```
   private ObservableCollection<DataClass> myTasks;
   ```

8. Next, add the method `IntializeList`, which will query the data collection class and return the results. The result from the query is databound to a list box control's `ItemsSource`:

   ```
   private void InitalizeList()
   {
     string selectQuery = "Select * from MyTasks";
     myTasks = (Application.Current as App).
       db.SelectObservableCollection<DataClass>(selectQuery);
     lstTasks.ItemsSource = myTasks;
   }
   ```

9. In the `Main_Loaded` event, call the method `InitializeList()`.

10. Press *F5* and run to see the resulting listing from the local database, as shown in the following screenshot:

11. Now we shall update using the form. Open the `.cs` file, and replace the `Add_Click` method, as follows:

```
private void btnAdd_Click(object sender, RoutedEventArgs e)
{
    DateTime createdDate = DateTime.Now;
    int rec;
    string strInsert = "Insert into MyTasks values
        (@Name,@Notes,@Priority, @DateDue)";

    MyTasks newTask = new MyTasks
```

```
    {
      Name = txtName.Text.ToString(),
      Notes = txtNotes.Text.ToString(),
      Priority = txtPriority.Text.ToString(),
      DateDue = DateTime.Parse(txtPrioirty.Text.ToString());
    };

    rec = (Application.Current as App).db.Insert
      <MyTasks>(newTask, strInsert);

}
```

12. Press *F5* and run again. Now you can add the new task to the database.

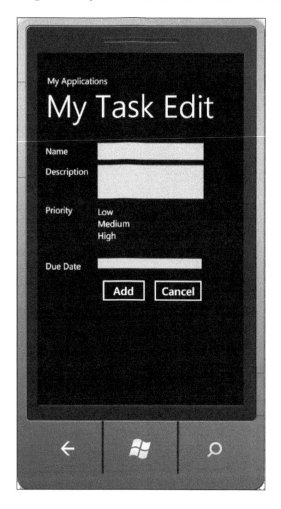

How it works...

We initially loaded the database file using the `DBHelper` class. Then, we used the `select` query and executed it to return the results. The list is then assigned to a list box for display. Once we have the list displayed, we then add the code to insert the task using the form. Here we used an `insert` SQL statement.

This recipe demonstrates how easy it is to implement the popular SQLite database as an embedded database in your apps. You can reuse SQLite across other mobile platforms as well. So this makes the SQLite a very portable solution for multiple platforms.

See also

Check the following recipe to see how SQL CE is used as an embedded database. In the following two recipes, we discuss other options available as local database storage. Also, check *Chapter 7, Windows Communication Framework - WCF*, which discusses how to store the data externally.

SQL CE as a local store

In this recipe, let's explore how we can use SQL CE—an embedded database from Microsoft—as a local store. Some of the features of SQL CE are as follows:

- ▶ It is totally free without any license restrictions.
- ▶ Embedded database means you don't even need to install in order access the database; you can just copy the binary into the project folder and use it like a file.
- ▶ There are two ways to use the SQL CE in Phone applications; one is as a device storage, which allows read/write access, and the other is as an App storage, which allows read-only access. A scenario for the App storage is when you want to ship something like dictionary data or searchable data that doesn't need to be updated by the user.
- ▶ It is supported by Visual Studio for creating and editing databases. Also, you can modify indexes.
- ▶ You can use **Entity Framework** (**EF**) to create the model code. WP7 applications only support LINQ to SQL for now.

Getting ready

First, you need to make sure you download and install Visual Studio 2010 SP1. Once this is successful, download **SQL CE Tools** for Visual Studio 2010 SP1 at the following address: `http://go.microsoft.com/fwlink/?LinkId=212219`.

Next, download SQL Server 2008 R2 Express from the following address: `http://www.microsoft.com/express/Database/`. SQL Server 2008 R2 Express allows you to open the SQL CE database files for viewing and editing. You can perform these tasks within the Visual Studio Environment as well. Launch the SQL Server Management Studio.

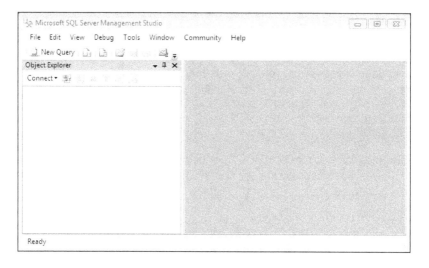

How to do it...

In this recipe, we will learn how to use the SQL Server Management Studio to create an SQL CE database file as well as a basic `MyTask` table with different columns in it. Once the table is created, we use SQL `insert` statements to add a couple of sample records to the table.

1. Let's create a new compact database from the **Connect** dropdown using the SQL Server Management Studio.

2. SQL CE databases have file extensions of `.sdf`.

3. Navigate to the **Database file** dropdown and select **New database**, then enter the name `mytasks` for the database and enter the **Login** as `Admin` and a password you can remember.

4. SQL CE is an embeded database so we can save it to local folder with a filename just like you would create any other file. We can copy and send it in an e-mail or upload it to a server. It is this flexibility that makes SQL CE very desirable for smart phone apps as local storage.

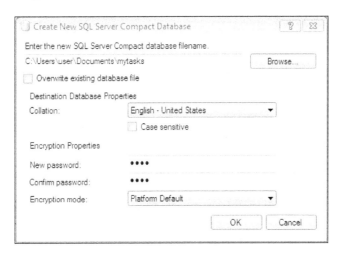

5. Now open the `mytasks.sdf` database.

6. Add a new table called `MyTasks`.

7. Let's add all the data fields we used in the *Chapter 1* MyTasks app recipe. Id is the new Primary Key we added to the table. Add Name, Notes, Priority, DueDate, and DateCreated columns to the MyTasks table.

8. We used nvarchar for Name, Notes, and Priority with different lengths. We used datetime for the DueDate and DateCreated columns.

9. We can also set different defaults for each column, like we can set the Id column as identity with an **Identity Increment** and **Identity Seed**, as shown in the following screenshot:

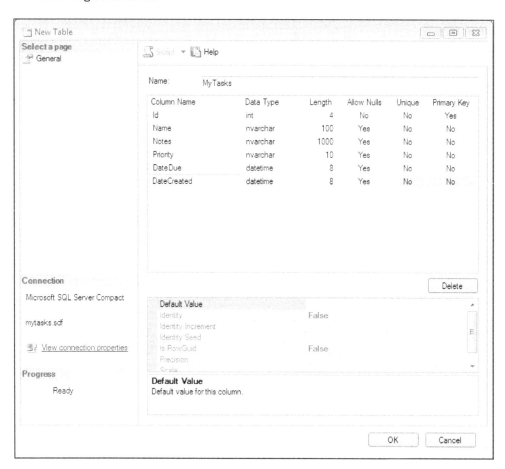

10. Once the table is created, let's add a couple of test data rows using SQL insert statements.

```
insert into MyTasks values (1,'Task Name 1', 'Task Note 1',
    'High','9/1/2011',getdate());
insert into MyTasks values (2,'Task Name 2', 'Task Note 2',
    'High','9/1/2011',getdate());
```

11. Click on the **New Query** icon in the tab bar and then **Execute** the selected query. You should get the result shown in the following screenshot:

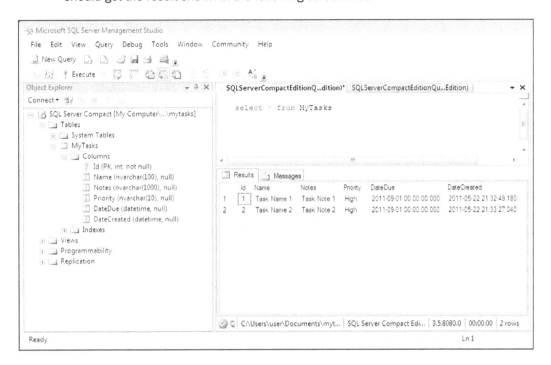

How it works...

We created a new database file and a new table MyTasks. We then added all the columns needed for the MyTasks app to the table. Next, we inserted a couple of test data rows into the table using SQL insert statements.

Finally, we used a select statement to query the data in the MyTasks tables. We just looked at how easy and similar SQL CE is to other database options. We can also use inline SQL statements to store the data locally.

In order to use this in a WP7 project, you should include this as your project resource. Once it is part of the project you can access the database using LINQ to SQL. You will be accessing the file stored in the installation folder using the following connection string:

```
String conn = "Data Source = 'appdata:/mydb.sdf';
   File Mode = read only;"

"appdata:/" indicates that file resides in the installation
   folder within the XAP file and it is read only.
```

There's more...

The SQL CE solution is very flexible and powerful. We can build scalable apps using SQL CE, as it is supported in the ASP.NET environment too and can be easily upgraded to SQL Server or SQL Azure (Microsoft Cloud Service).

Creating and deleting data in SQL CE using LINQ to SQL

In this section, we will create a sample recipe that will create the local database and the table `MyTask`. Using the `Context` object, we can use LINQ to SQL to query the table or we can perform a standard *CRUD* operation on the `MyTask` table.

1. Open the new project and create a new **Phone Application**. Name it `Ch5_MyTasks_SqlCE`.

2. Open `MainPage.xaml` and add a button control and list box control, as shown in the following code snippet, inside the `ContentPanel`. In the `ListBox DataTemplate`, add four `TextBlock` controls and set the binding properties to `Name`, `DateDue`, `Priority`, and `Notes` respectively:

```
<!--ContentPanel - place additional content here-->
<Grid x:Name="ContentPanel" Grid.Row="1" Margin="12,0,12,0">
  <Button x:Name="Button1" Content="Create Sample Records"
    VerticalAlignment="Top"  Click="Button1_Click"/>
  <ListBox x:Name ="lstTasks" Margin="0,78,0,0">
    <ListBox.ItemTemplate>
      <DataTemplate>
        <Grid>
          <Grid.RowDefinitions>
            <RowDefinition />
            <RowDefinition />
            <RowDefinition Height="15" />
          </Grid.RowDefinitions>

          <Grid.ColumnDefinitions>
            <ColumnDefinition Width="150" />
            <ColumnDefinition Width="200" />
            <ColumnDefinition Width="100" />
          </Grid.ColumnDefinitions>

          <TextBlock Grid.Row="0" Grid.Column="0" Text="
            {Binding Name}" FontWeight="Bold"
            Foreground="OrangeRed"/>
          <TextBlock Grid.Row="0" Grid.Column="1" Text="
            {Binding DateDue}" />
          <TextBlock Grid.Row="0" Grid.Column="2" Text="
            {Binding Priority}"  Foreground="Yellow"/>
```

```xml
            <TextBlock Grid.Row="1" Grid.ColumnSpan="3"
              Text="{Binding Notes}" />
            <TextBlock Grid.Row="2" Grid.ColumnSpan="3" />
          </Grid>
        </DataTemplate>
      </ListBox.ItemTemplate>
    </ListBox>
  </Grid>
```

3. Right-click the project reference folder and add a reference to the assembly `System.Data.Linq` and then add the following three `using` declaratives at the top of the page:

```csharp
using System.Data.Linq;
using System.Data.Linq.Mapping;
using Microsoft.Phone.Data.Linq.Mapping;
```

4. Open the `MainPage.xaml.cs` file, add the `MyTask` class, which will be used for creating the `MyTask` table with all the column properties. Set the Column Attribute **IsPrimaryKey** to true for property **Id**. This property will be created as Primary Key in the database table, as follows:

```csharp
[Table]
public class MyTask
{
  [Column(IsPrimaryKey = true)]
  public int Id { get; set; }
  [Column]
  public string Name { get; set; }
  [Column]
  public string Notes { get; set; }
  [Column]
  public string Priority { get; set; }
  [Column]
  public DateTime DateDue { get; set; }
  [Column]
  public DateTime DateCreated { get; set; }
}
```

5. Next, add the `MyDataContext` class that is inherited from `DataContext`. In this class, we will initialize the table as `MyTaskItems` with `MyTask` class, as follows:

```csharp
public class MyDataContext : DataContext
{
            public Table<MyTask> MyTaskItems;

  public MyDataContext(string connection)
    : base(connection) { }
}
```

6. Now, we will initialize `MyDataContext` in the `MainPage` constructor with the database name `MyTaskDb.sdf`, as shown in the following code snippet. `isostore:/` points to a device storage that has read and write capabilities. After the initialization, we check if the database file exists. If it is not true, then create the database using the method `CreateDatabase()`:

```
// Constructor
public MainPage()
{
  InitializeComponent();

  MyDataContext db = new MyDataContext("isostore:/MyTaskDB.sdf");
  if (!db.DatabaseExists())
    db.CreateDatabase();
}
```

7. Next, add a method to display records in the database and bind the results to the list box's `ItemsSource`. These steps are shown in the following code snippet:

```
public void MainPage_Loaded(object sender,
  RoutedEventArgs e)
{
  ShowRecords();
}

private void ShowRecords()
{
  MyDataContext db = new MyDataContext("isostore:/MyTaskDB.sdf");
  var q = from b in db.MyTaskItems
    orderby b.Name
    select b;

  List<MyTask> myData = q.ToList();
  lstTasks.ItemsSource = myData;
}
```

8. Add the `DeleteRecords` method so that we can clean the table every time we create the sample data. In this method, we open the database using `MyDataContext` class and then we use a LINQ statement to query the database for table `MyTaskItems`. For each row we will call the `DeleteOnSumbit` method to delete the record, as follows:

```
private void DeleteRecords()
{
  MyDataContext db = new MyDataContext("isostore:/MyTaskDB.sdf");
  var q = from b in db.MyTaskItems
    select b;
  foreach (MyTask taskItem in q)
```

```
  {
    db.MyTaskItems.DeleteOnSubmit(taskItem);
  }
  db.SubmitChanges();
}
```

9. Now we shall add a button click event, which will have the code to insert sample records into the database. Before we insert the sample records we call the `DeleteRecords` method to delete any data in the table so that we can insert the sample data. Here we open the database and using the object initializers we create a couple of rows using the `InsertOnSubmit` method. After inserting, we call the `ShowRecords()` method to display the rows in the table:

```
private void Button1_Click(object sender, RoutedEventArgs e)
{
//let's delete any records so we can recreate the sample data
  DeleteRecords();

  MyDataContext db = new MyDataContext("isostore:/MyTaskDB.sdf");

  MyTask myData = new MyTask()
  {
    Id = 1,
    Name = "Task Name 1",
    Notes = "Task Notes 1",
    Priority = "Low",
    DateDue = DateTime.Parse("10/01/2011"),
    DateCreated = DateTime.Parse("11/01/2011")
  };

  db.MyTaskItems.InsertOnSubmit(myData);

  myData = new MyTask()
  {
    Id = 2,
    Name = "Task Name 2",
    Notes = " Task Notes 2",
    Priority = "High",
    DateDue = DateTime.Parse("11/11/2011"),
    DateCreated = DateTime.Parse("10/11/2011")
  };

  db.MyTaskItems.InsertOnSubmit(myData);

  db.SubmitChanges();

  ShowRecords();
}
```

10. Press *F5*. You should see the empty page with two buttons as shown in the following screenshot:

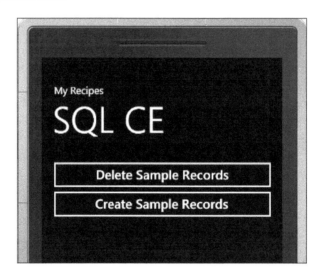

11. Click on the **Create Sample Records** button to create a couple of sample data records and display the results as shown in the following screenshot. You can also try deleting the sample records and recreating them again.

See also

SQL CE is similar to SQLite Client, so check the recipe *SQLite Client as an embedded database* in this chapter. Check the recipes in *Chapter 6* and *Chapter 7* for details on how to use web services to save data on remote servers. Also, check the following important links to get more information from MSDN:

- ▸ LINQ to SQL Support for Windows Phone:

  `http://msdn.microsoft.com/en-us/library/hh202872(v=VS.92).aspx`

- ▸ Local Database Overview for Windows Phone:

  `http://msdn.microsoft.com/en-us/library/hh202860(v=VS.92).aspx`

- ▸ Local Database Connection Strings for Windows Phone:

  `http://msdn.microsoft.com/en-us/library/hh202861(v=VS.92).aspx`

McObject Perst as an embedded object database

In this recipe we will discuss how to use the third-party embedded database from McObject called Perst.

Getting ready

Download Perst.NET from `http://www.mcobject.com`. You have to first register to get the download option. After you download it to your local machine, unzip, and save it to the local folder for later reference with a folder name `Perst.Net`.

Navigate to the saved folder and open the `PerstWP7` project and build the project. We need the `PerstWP7.dll` to be added to our recipe demo. Now let's build an app similar to our first `MyTasks` recipe in *Chapter 1*. First add a reference to `PerstWP7` to the project reference.

How to do it...

In this recipe we will learn how we can use the Perst Database to implement our `MyTask` sample.

1. Copy the `MyTasks` project we created from *Chapter 1* and rename it `MyTasks_Perst`

2. Open `App.xaml.cs` and add the initalization code for the Perst Database, as follows:

```
public Database Database { get; internal set; }

internal void OpenPerstDatabase()
{
  using (var stor = IsolatedStorageFile.
    GetUserStoreForApplication())
  {
    if (stor.FileExists(DataGenerator.StorageName))
    {
      InitializePerstStorage();
    }
  }
}

internal void ClosePerstDatabase()
{
  if (Database != null && Database.Storage != null)
    Database.Storage.Close();
}

// Code to execute when the application is launching
  (eg, from Start)
// This code will not execute when the application is reactivated
private void Application_Launching(object sender,
  LaunchingEventArgs e)
{
  OpenPerstDatabase();
}

// Code to execute when the application is activated
  (brought to foreground)
// This code will not execute when the application
  is first launched
private void Application_Activated(object sender,
  ActivatedEventArgs e)
{
  OpenPerstDatabase();
}

// Code to execute when the application is deactivated
  (sent to background)
// This code will not execute when the application is closing
private void Application_Deactivated(object sender,
  DeactivatedEventArgs e)
```

```
{
  ClosePerstDatabase();
}

// Code to execute when the application is closing (eg, user
  hit Back)
// This code will not execute when the application is deactivated
private void Application_Closing(object sender,
  ClosingEventArgs e)
{
  ClosePerstDatabase();
}

internal void InitializePerstStorage()
{
  var storage = StorageFactory.Instance.CreateStorage();
 // Creating Instance of Perst Storage
  storage.SetProperty("perst.file.extension.quantum", 512 * 1024);
// Initial Size set 512KB
  storage.SetProperty("perst.extension.quantum", 256 * 1024);
// Step of storage extension 256KB

  storage.Open("MyTaskDB.dbs", 0); // Open Storage

  //Create Database wrapper over Perst Storage
  Database = new Database(storage, false, true, new
  FullTextSearchHelper(storage));
  Database.EnableAutoIndices = false; //Turn off auto-index
    creation (defined manually)
```

3. `MainPage.xaml` should look exactly the same but the data list is retrieved from the local Perst database. Please refer to the *Chapter 1* `MyTasks` recipe for more information. Let's replace the `InitializeTasks` method with the following:

```
private void InitializeTasks()
{
  myTasks = (from c in Database.GetTable<MyTasks>()
    select c).ToArray();

}
```

4. Now implement the **Add New Task** form similar to that in the *Chapter 1* `MyTasks` recipe. You can also add tasks by saving the task object.

How it works...

First, we initialize `MyTaskDB.dbs` in the `ApplicationStartup` event handler. We check if the file exists; if yes then we call the `InitializePerstStorage` method.

Unlike with a relational database, we don't need to create any tables in the Perst database as each object can be stored individually. This can be achieved by inheriting the model class or `MyTasks` class from the `Persistent` class. We can also make the other fields full-text searchable by using `attribute`. We can then save the form using the `save()` method.

There's more...

We can implement more features like Search and Delete options. Please refer to McObject's website to get the latest update and read the tutorial provided on the website for more information. Here is the link for documentation:

```
http://www.mcobject.com/index.cfm?fuseaction=download&pageid=642&sect
ionid=139
```

See also

Check the preceding recipe *SQL CE as a local store*, which is a Microsoft supported database option. Also, check *Chapter 8* for how to use the MVVM (Model View ViewModel) pattern in your application to develop a more maintainable and scalable app.

6
Representational State Transfer—REST

In this chapter, we will cover:

- ▶ Consuming RSS feeds
- ▶ Using the Twitter API
- ▶ Building a simple REST service

Introduction

The beauty of the World Wide Web is its simplicity in addressing any resource using a simple **URI (Uniform Resource Identifier)** wherever it exists or whatever type it may be. This architectural success is the basis of **Representational State Transfer** (**REST**).

HTTP (Hypertext Transfer Protocol) is the most simple, scalable, stateless, and open protocol used on the Web. The two most popular verbs used are GET and POST. GET returns a specific resource requested, while POST creates a new resource. REST services provide simple URI access to resources exposed over HTTP. REST supports four HTTP verbs: GET, POST, PUT, and DELETE. Unlike POST, PUT modifies an existing resource. DELETE removes the resource. In this chapter let's explore different providers such as CNN and Twitter, and build a simple REST service.

Different types of content or media are available like the following popular ones:

- ▶ XML – application/xml
- ▶ RSS – application/rss+xml
- ▶ ATOM – application/atom+xml
- ▶ JSON – application/json
- ▶ XHTML – application/xhtml

WebClient and HttpWebRequest are two important classes used in Windows Phone 7 to request services. The following picture illustrates how it works at a high level.

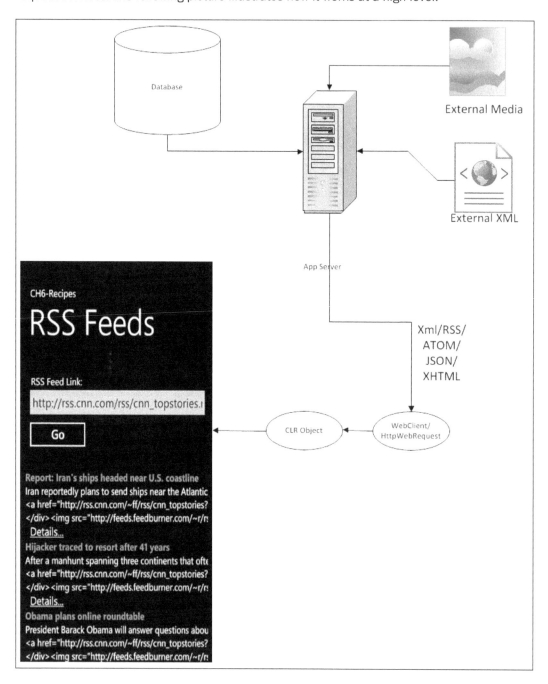

Consuming RSS Feeds

In this recipe, we will learn how to consume RSS feeds. **RSS (Really Simple Syndication)** feeds are published by many news agencies and informational websites such as CNN. RSS/ATOM is also used extensively in publishing blogs. RSS is based on XML format.

Getting ready

Let's try to check what is published at a CNN feed first. There are many feeds available at CNN. We will use one feed that returns the *Top Stories*. Check the following URL: `http://rss.cnn.com/rss/cnn_topstories.rss`. You should get content similar to that shown in the following screenshot, which contains the name of the top story with a link, posted date, and short description:

> **Current Feed Content**
>
> ❖ **Senate GOP proposes fallback option in debt impasse**
> Posted: Tue, 12 Jul 2011 19:59:17 EDT
> Senate Republicans offered a plan that would give President Obama power to raise the debt ceiling, but would require three votes in Congress before the election.

The following is the partial XML feed:

```
<?xml-stylesheet type="text/xsl" media="screen"
  href="/~d/styles/rss2full.xsl"?>
<?xml-stylesheet type="text/css" media="screen"
  href="http://rss.cnn.com/~d/styles/itemcontent.css"?>
<rss xmlns:media="http://search.yahoo.com/mrss/"
  xmlns:feedburner="http://rssnamespace.org/feedburner/ext/1.0"
  version="2.0">
<channel>
  <title>CNN.com</title>
  <link>http://www.cnn.com/?eref=rss_topstories</link>
  <description>CNN.com delivers up-to-the-minute news and information
    on the latest top stories, weather, entertainment, politics and
    more.</description>
  <language>en-us</language>
  <copyright>⊠ 2011 Cable News Network LP, LLLP.</copyright>
  <pubDate>Sun, 24 Jul 2011 23:16:13 EDT</pubDate>
  <ttl>5</ttl>
  <image>
    <title>CNN.com</title>
    <link>http://www.cnn.com/?eref=rss_topstories</link>
    <url>http://i2.cdn.turner.com/cnn/.element/img/1.0/logo/
      cnn.logo.rss.gif</url>
```

```
<width>144</width>
<height>33</height>
<description>CNN.com delivers up-to-the-minute news and
    information on the latest top stories, weather, entertainment,
    politics and more.</description>
</image>
...
...
```

How to do it...

In this recipe, we will create an application that will have a textbox to collect any RSS feed link and display the updates from the feed provider. Also, when you click the item in the list box you will be directed to the site to display the details.

1. Open a new project and create a new **Phone 7 Application** with the name `Recipe1_ RssReader`.

2. Add a new class to the project with the name `RssFeed.cs`. Open the file and add a new class `RssFeed` to collect the feed data:

```
public class RssFeed
{
  public string Title { get; set; }
  public string Content { get; set; }
  public DateTime DatePosted { get; set; }
  public Uri URL { get; set; }
}
```

3. Open the `MainPage.xaml` file and add three rows with two `TextBlock` controls and a `HyperlinkButton`:

```
<Grid x:Name="ContentPanel2" Margin="12,217,12,-13" Grid.Row="1">
  <ListBox x:Name ="lstItems" Margin="0,6,0,0">
    <ListBox.ItemTemplate>
      <DataTemplate>
        <Grid>
          <Grid.RowDefinitions>
            <RowDefinition />
            <RowDefinition />
            <RowDefinition />
          </Grid.RowDefinitions>

          <StackPanel VerticalAlignment="Top">
            <TextBlock Grid.Row="0" Text="{Binding Title}"
              FontWeight="Bold" Foreground="OrangeRed"/>
            <TextBlock Grid.Row="1"  Text="{Binding Content}" />
```

```
        <HyperlinkButton TargetName="_blank" Grid.Row="2"
          Name="DetailLink" Content="Details..."
          NavigateUri="{Binding URL}" Foreground="Yellow"
          HorizontalAlignment="Left"/>

      </StackPanel>
    </Grid>
  </DataTemplate>
</ListBox.ItemTemplate>
</ListBox>
</Grid>
```

4. Open the `MainPage.xaml.cs` file. As we are going to use LINQ to XML, let's add a reference to the assembly `System.Xml.Linq` to the project, and then add the `using` declarative at the beginning of the file:

```
using System.Xml.Linq;
```

5. Add code to initialize the `WebClient` object and the `DownloadStringCompleted` event handler as shown in the following partial code snippet:

```
public partial class MainPage : PhoneApplicationPage
{
  // Constructor
  WebClient remoteXml;
  public MainPage()
  {
    InitializeComponent();

    remoteXml = new WebClient();
    remoteXml.DownloadStringCompleted += new
      DownloadStringCompletedEventHandler
      (remoteXml_DownloadStringCompleted);
  }

  ...
```

6. Now add the `DownloadStringCompleted` event method. In this method, we download the XML file into the `XDocument` object and then using LINQ to XML we parse the three elements we need to save:

```
private void remoteXml_DownloadStringCompleted(object sender,
  DownloadStringCompletedEventArgs e)
{
  if (e.Error != null)
    return;
  XDocument xdoc = XDocument.Parse(e.Result);

  List<RssFeed> rssFeeds;
```

```
rssFeeds = (from item in xdoc.Descendants("item")
  select new RssFeed()
{
  Title = item.Element("title").Value,
  Content = item.Element("description").Value,
  URL = new Uri(item.Element("link").Value, UriKind.Absolute),
}).ToList();
  lstItems.ItemsSource = rssFeeds;
}
```

7. Now add the button event handler to navigate to the feed URL:

```
private void button1_Click(object sender, RoutedEventArgs e)
{
  string txtUri = textBox1.Text;
  txtUri = Uri.EscapeUriString(txtUri);
  Uri uri = new Uri(txtUri,UriKind.Absolute);
  remoteXml.DownloadStringAsync(uri);
}
```

8. Press *F5* and as we have embedded a CNN feed link, just click on **Go** and you should see the top stories feed displayed:

9. Click on **Details** to launch the browser in order to see the details of the news item you selected from the feed items online.

How it works...

For navigating to RSS feeds, we basically have two choices in Phone 7: one is by using the `WebClient` and the other is `HttpWebRequest`. Here we use the `WebClient`.

In the `DownloadStringCompleted` method, we use `XDocument` to parse the remote RSS feed XML file. Once it is downloaded, we parse the XML using a LINQ to XML query. Based on the feed XML, we just collected three elements: title, description, and link.

There's more...

For more information on the `WebClient` class check this MSDN site:
`http://msdn.microsoft.com/en-us/library/system.net.webclient(v=VS.95).aspx`.

Refer to *Chapter 7* on **MVVM** (**Model View ViewModel**) to build scalable and flexible applications. Also, check *Chapter 3* on XML to learn more scenarios where XML is being used.

Using the Twitter API

In this recipe, let's build a Twitter client app using the Twitter API. This is similar to the previous RSS reader recipe. Here, instead of RSS format you will receive the custom XML format related to the Twitter username or screen name.

Getting ready

First study the Twitter API resource page at:

```
https://dev.twitter.com/docs/api
```

There are many categories of API available such as Timelines, Tweets, Search, and so on. We will be using `statuses/user_timeline` for a given user in this recipe.

How to do it...

In the next steps, we will create a client application, which will have a textbox to search for a name and return the latest updates for that username.

1. Open a new project and create a new **Phone 7 Application** with the name `Recipe2_ TwiitterClient`.

2. Right-click on the project folder and add a new class to the `TwitterFeed.cs` file. Open the file and add the new class to store the Twitter feed information. We will have one string variable called `Content`:

   ```
   public class TwitterFeed
   {
     public string Content { get; set; }
   }
   ```

3. Open the `MainPage.xaml` file and change the `ApplicationTitle` and `PageTitle`:

   ```
   <!--TitlePanel contains the name of the application and page
       title-->
   <StackPanel x:Name="TitlePanel" Grid.Row="0" Margin="12,17,0,28">
     <TextBlock x:Name="ApplicationTitle" Text="CH6-Recipes"
       Style="{StaticResource PhoneTextNormalStyle}"/>
   ```

```
    <TextBlock x:Name="PageTitle" Text="Twitter Client" Margin="9,-
      7,0,0" Style="{StaticResource PhoneTextTitle1Style}"/>
  </StackPanel>
```

4. Add the `Search TextBlock` and a `TextBox` following it:

```
<!--ContentPanel - place additional content here-->
<Grid x:Name="ContentPanel" Grid.Row="1" Margin="12,0,12,0">
  <TextBox Height="72" HorizontalAlignment="Left"
    Margin="0,52,0,0" Name="textBox1" Text="BillGates"
    VerticalAlignment="Top" Width="460" />
  <TextBlock Height="30" HorizontalAlignment="Left"
    Margin="14,32,0,0" Name="textBlock1" Text="Search:"
    VerticalAlignment="Top" />
  <Button Content="Go" Height="72" HorizontalAlignment="Left"
    Margin="0,116,0,0" Name="button1" VerticalAlignment="Top"
    Width="160" Click="button1_Click" />
</Grid>
```

5. Now add a `ListBox` along with a `TextBlock` inside the `Grid` control
    "`ContentPanel2`":

```
<Grid x:Name="ContentPanel2" Margin="12,217,12,-13" Grid.Row="1">
  <ListBox x:Name ="lstItems" Margin="0,6,0,0">
    <ListBox.ItemTemplate>
      <DataTemplate>
        <Grid>
          <Grid.RowDefinitions>
            <RowDefinition />
            <RowDefinition Height="20"/>
          </Grid.RowDefinitions>

          <StackPanel VerticalAlignment="Top">
            <TextBlock Grid.Row="0" Text="{Binding Content}"/>
            <TextBlock Grid.Row="1"  />
          </StackPanel>
        </Grid>
      </DataTemplate>
    </ListBox.ItemTemplate>
  </ListBox>
</Grid>
```

6. Open the `MainPage.xaml.cs` file and add the following code using the `WebClient`
    class and then `DownloadStringCompletedEventHandler`:

```
public partial class MainPage : PhoneApplicationPage
{
  // Constructor
```

```
WebClient remoteXml;
public MainPage()
{
  InitializeComponent();

  remoteXml = new WebClient();
  remoteXml.DownloadStringCompleted += new
    DownloadStringCompletedEventHandler
    (remoteXml_DownloadStringCompleted);
}


private void remoteXml_DownloadStringCompleted(object sender,
  DownloadStringCompletedEventArgs e)
{
  if (e.Error != null)
    return;
  XDocument xdoc = XDocument.Parse(e.Result);

  List<TwitterFeed> tweets;

  tweets = (from entry in xdoc.Descendants("status")
    select new TwitterFeed()
    {
      Content = entry.Element("text").Value,
}).ToList();

  lstItems.ItemsSource = tweets;
}
```

7. Add the button click event for **Go**. In this method, we will hard-code the Twitter API URL for user timeline. In the query string, we will append the Twitter username, which we get from the textbox. Then, we will call `DownloadStringAsync` to navigate to the URL passed:

```
private void button1_Click(object sender, RoutedEventArgs e)
{
  string txtSearch = textBox1.Text;

  string txtUri = "http://api.twitter.com//1/statuses/
    user_timeline.xml?screen_name=" + txtSearch;

  Uri uri = new Uri(txtUri, UriKind.Absolute);
  remoteXml.DownloadStringAsync(uri);
}
```

8. Press *F5* and you should get the search textbox with the **Go** button. Type in the Twitter username or screen name. When you click on **Go**, you should see all the User Tweets:

How it works...

In the preceding recipe, you got the standard RSS formatted XML, which is similar across all RSS feeds. Here twitter provides its own set of APIs to provide different XML content. One such API is user timeline, which takes the input `screen_name` and returns all the tweet updates for that user.

We used the `WebClient` class to navigate and download the results of the API call. In the `DownloadStringCompleted` event method, we used LINQ to XML. Here we parsed the returned XML file into the `XDocument` object and then queried the XML document for `text` nodes.

There's more...

In this recipe, you understood how simple it is to call any REST API, download the result, and save it in local objects. You can refer to the Twitter API reference document to build a robust client app.

See also

Check the first recipe titled *Consuming RSS Feeds*. Also check the following recipe to learn how to build your own REST service.

Building a simple REST service

In the last two recipes, we understood how to call simple REST-based web services using `WebClient` classes. In this recipe, let's build a simple REST service and a client to understand how easy and simple the REST architecture is. We will use the WebMatrix to build the web service and stream the result using **JSON** (**Java Script Object Notation**) format.

Getting ready

To create the web service we will be using Microsoft's WebMatrix tool, as it is a simple and a free tool for building server-side applications. Install it using the Platform Installer at this location: `http://www.asp.net/web-pages`.

How to do it...

Let's build a simple MyLinks service using the WebMatrix and MyLinks client using the Phone 7 application to consume the service.

1. Open the WebMatrix and create a website using a blank template and name it **MyLinks** site, as shown in the following screenshot:

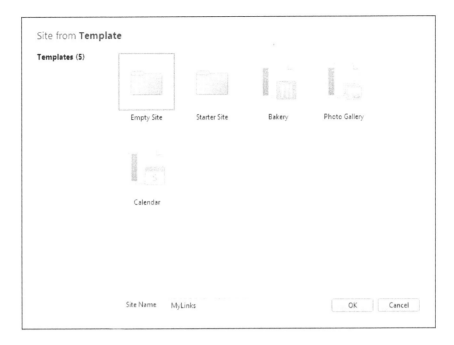

2. Click on **Databases** from the Navigation bar at the bottom to add a local database. The local database has a file extension of .sdf, which means that it is file-based. Hence it can be saved to the App_Data folder and consumed using a simple SQL query. Name the database file MyLinks.sdf.

3. Right-click on the **MyLinks.sdf** file and add a new table called **Link**. Now add three columns Id, Name, and Url, where Id is the Primary Key, Name is text (ntext) and Url a string (nvarchar). When you are done, the table structure should look like the following screenshot:

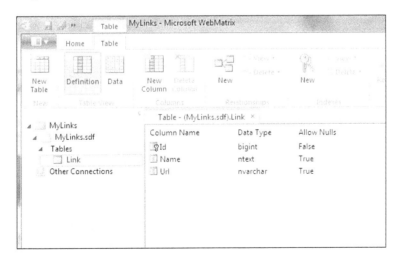

4. Now right-click on the table **Link** and select **Data**. Add three sample rows, as follows:

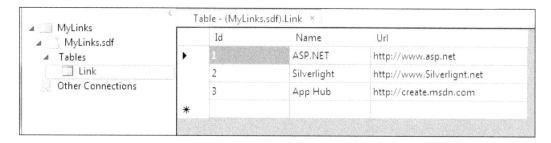

5. Using the Files Navigation bar at the bottom of the screen, add a new folder and name it `App_Data`. Then add a new file and name it `MyLib.cshtml`, which is a `Razor` syntax-supported file. `Razor` is built on top of ASP.NET to make it faster at building quick server-side code and combining it with the HTML syntax easily.

6. Open the `MyLib.cshtml` file and delete all the default HTML code in it. Now let's add the Razor syntax for functions, which is `@functions {}`. When adding the methods to `@functions` you can reference them to any files on the website.

7. Add the `MyLink` class to hold the information for `Id`, `Name`, and `URL`:

    ```
    @functions{
       public class MyLink
       public long Id {get; set;}
       public string Name {get;set;}
       public string Url {get; set;}
    }
    ```

8. Now add a public static function call `GetLink`, which will return a specific record from the database using a `select` statement.

    ```
    public static MyLink GetLink(int id)
    {
      MyLink myLink = new MyLink();
      var query = "Select * from Link where Id=" + id;
      var db = Database.Open("MyLinks");

      var rlink = db.QuerySingle(query);
      myLink.Id = rlink.Id;
      myLink.Name = rlink.Name;
      myLink.Url = rlink.Url;

      return myLink;
    }
    ```

9. Now add another file called `Default.cshtml`. This is your index file for the site. In this we will call the function we created to test our connection to the database and display the result:

```
<!DOCTYPE html>
@{
   var myLink = MyLib.GetLink(1);
}
<html lang="en">
  <head>
    <meta charset="utf-8" />
    <title>My Link</title>
  </head>
  <body>
    <ul>
       <li>@myLink.Name</li>
       <li>@myLink.Url</li>
    </ul>

  </body>
</html>
```

10. Click on **Run** at the top icon bar. You should get the result from the first row in the **Link** table:

11. Now let's add another C Sharp `Razor` file to the project and call it `mylinkservice.cshtml`. Remove all the default HTML code in this file. In this file, we are expecting the client to call the service with query string `id`. We will check if the `id` is null or not. If it is not null, then we will reference the `MyLib.GetLink` method and pass the `id` as the parameter:

```
@{
   string id = Request.QueryString["id"];
   if(id != null)
   {
      var myLink = MyLib.GetLink(int.Parse(id));
```

```
    Json.Write(myLink,Response.Output);
  }
  else
  {
    Response.Write("Expects a parameter id in querystring,
      please try again");
  }
}
```

12. Razor has a helper function to stream the object to the client using the JSON format.

13. We can test the service by running the project while selecting `mylinkservice.cshtml`. Pass the query string as `id = 2` to test the REST service. You should get the result in JSON format with a name and value pair. Open the browser and navigate to the following link:

    `http://localhost:64303/mylinkservice.cshtml?id=2`

14. Now let's build the Phone 7 Application to consume this service. Open a new project and create the project using the Phone 7 application template. Call this project `Recipe3_MyLinksClient`.

15. Right-click on the project and add the class file. Name this file `MyLink.cs` and add the `MyLink` class to it:

```
namespace Recipe3_MyLinksClient
{
  public class MyLink
  {
    public long Id { get; set; }
    public string Name { get; set; }
    public string Url { get; set; }
  }
}
```

16. Open the `MainPage.xaml` file and change the `ApplicationTitle` and the `PageTitle`.

```
<!--TitlePanel contains the name of the application and page
  title-->
```

```
<StackPanel x:Name="TitlePanel" Grid.Row="0" Margin="12,17,0,28">
  <TextBlock x:Name="ApplicationTitle" Text="CH6-Recipes"
    Style="{StaticResource PhoneTextNormalStyle}"/>
  <TextBlock x:Name="PageTitle" Text="MyLinks Client" Margin="9,-
    7,0,0" Style="{StaticResource PhoneTextTitle1Style}"/>
</StackPanel>
```

17. Add the following controls so we can supply different values for `id` and display the result we get from the service:

```
<!--TitlePanel contains the name of the application and page
  title-->
<StackPanel x:Name="TitlePanel" Grid.Row="0" Margin="12,17,0,28">
  <TextBlock x:Name="ApplicationTitle" Text="CH6-Recipes"
    Style="{StaticResource PhoneTextNormalStyle}"/>
  <TextBlock x:Name="PageTitle" Text="MyLinks Client" Margin="9,-
    7,0,0" Style="{StaticResource PhoneTextTitle1Style}"/>
</StackPanel>

<!--ContentPanel - place additional content here-->
<Grid x:Name="ContentPanel" Grid.Row="1" Margin="12,0,12,0">

  <TextBox Height="72" HorizontalAlignment="Left"
    Margin="0,52,0,0" Name="textBox1" Text="1"
    VerticalAlignment="Top" Width="460" />

  <TextBlock Height="30" HorizontalAlignment="Left"
    Margin="14,32,0,0" Name="textBlock1" Text="Link Id:"
    VerticalAlignment="Top" />

  <Button Content="Go" Height="72" HorizontalAlignment="Left"
    Margin="0,116,0,0" Name="button1" VerticalAlignment="Top"
    Width="160" Click="button1_Click" />
</Grid>

<Grid x:Name="ContentPanel2" Margin="12,217,12,-13"
  Grid.Row="1">
  <StackPanel VerticalAlignment="Top">
    <TextBlock Grid.Row="0" Name="LinkName" Text="Link Name"
      FontWeight="Bold" Foreground="OrangeRed"/>

    <TextBlock Grid.Row="1" Name="LinkUrl" Text="Link Url"
      FontWeight="Bold" Foreground="Yellow"/>
    <HyperlinkButton TargetName="_blank" Grid.Row="2"
      Name="LinkUrlNav" Content="Click here..." NavigateUri=""
      Foreground="Blue" HorizontalAlignment="Left"/>
  </StackPanel>
</Grid>
```

18. Open the `MainPage.xaml.cs` file. Unlike server side, we don't have any helper function for decoding JSON format. One choice we have is to use the class `DataContractJsonSerializer` in `System.Runtime.Serialization.Json`, which is in the assembly `System.Servicemodel.Web`. Right-click on the **Reference** folder and add a reference to the assembly `System.Servicemode.Web`, then add the following two `using` statements at the top:

```
using System.Runtime.Serialization.Json;
using System.IO;
```

19. Now, similar to our two preceding recipes, we will use the `WebClient` class to navigate to the `MyLinkService` URL. Here we will use `OpenReadAsync` instead of the `DownloadStringAsync` method:

```
public partial class MainPage : PhoneApplicationPage
{
  // Constructor
  WebClient remote;
  public MainPage()
  {
    InitializeComponent();

    remote = new WebClient();
    remote.OpenReadCompleted += new
      OpenReadCompletedEventHandler(remote_OpenReadCompleted);
  }

  private void remote_OpenReadCompleted(object sender,
    OpenReadCompletedEventArgs e)
  {
    if (e.Error != null)
      return;

    MyLink link = e.Result.Decode<MyLink>();

    LinkName.Text = link.Name.ToString();
    LinkUrl.Text = link.Url;
     LinkUrlNav.NavigateUri = new Uri(link.Url,UriKind.Absolute);
  }

  private void button1_Click(object sender, RoutedEventArgs e)
  {
    string txtUri = textBox1.Text;
    Uri uri = new
      Uri(@"http://localhost:64303/mylinkservice.cshtml?id=" +
      txtUri, UriKind.Absolute);
    remote.OpenReadAsync(uri);
  }

}
```

20. In the preceding code, we use `e.Result.Decode<MyLink>` to deserialize the `MyLink` object. This is achieved by using the `Extension` function to decode the JSON stream:

```
public static class JsonExtension
{
  // Source: Microsoft Sample for JSON Serialization
  public static T Decode<T>(this System.IO.Stream stream)
  {
    T obj = default(T);
    StreamReader sr = null;

    try
    {
      sr = new StreamReader(stream);
      string json = sr.ReadToEnd();
      var serializer = new DataContractJsonSerializer(typeof(T));
      obj = (T)serializer.ReadObject(stream);
    }
    finally
    {
      if (sr != null)
        sr.Close();
    }

    return obj;
  }
}
```

21. Press *F5* and enter a valid `id` for the link record. You should be able to retrieve the row information from the database through the REST service.

How it works...

In this recipe, we constructed a REST-based web service using simple and quick tools such as WebMatrix and Razor. In the first part we constructed a REST-based service using a simple URL and passed the query string as the parameter. We also connected to a local database to return the result, to show how we can not only return objects, but can also query the database for information in a simple URL syntax.

Once the REST service was built and tested, we constructed the Phone 7 client to consume it. Here we used the `WebClient` class as in our preceding recipes to navigate to the service URL and process the JSON formatted file. This recipe demonstrated how a JSON service can be built and consumed.

There's more...

In this recipe, we learned how to create a simple REST-based web service, which uses simple URLs to access the web service. Similarly, we can add insert, and update features to this service.

See also

Also check *Chapter 7* to understand how WCF can be used for building web services.

7
Windows Communication Framework—WCF

In this chapter we will cover:

- ▶ Writing and consuming a simple web service
- ▶ Building a service layer using WCF
- ▶ WCF using ADO.NET Entity Data Model
- ▶ LINQ to SQL

Introduction

Windows Communication Framework (**WCF**) is a unifying technology that includes various service technologies and provides one interface under one service. WCF is the Microsoft technology to realize the **Service Oriented Architecture** (**SOA**) vision. WCF is a very flexible technology that can be implemented as a Windows Service. It can be consumed by different clients like Windows forms, Silverlight applications, and ASP.NET pages.

This chapter will introduce how to create a service using WCF and then consume it in Phone 7 apps. We will cover different options available to access the data layer. We will learn how the **Entity Framework** or (**EF**) can be used and then LINQ to SQL technologies.

Writing and consuming a simple web service

In this recipe, let's create a simple web service using WCF and learn how to consume that service using a Phone 7 Client App.

Getting ready

Open the Visual Studio and create a new project from the template WCF Service and name it `Recipe1_SimpleService`. Delete the default files `Service1.svc` and `IService1.cs` from the project.

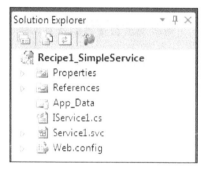

How to do it...

For this recipe, we will be creating two projects; one is a WCF Service application and the other one is a Windows Phone client application. In the Service application, we will add the service contract and operation contract. Then, we will add a simple method to return the service information. Once the service is built, we will consume that service in the Windows Phone client application to display what is returned by the method.

1. Right-click on the project and add a new item using the project template **WCF Service** and name this file `SimpleService.svc`. The project template automatically adds the `ISimpleService.cs` file, as shown in the following screenshot:

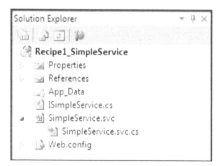

2. Open the `ISimpleService.cs` file and add two classes, one for the data contract and another for the service contract. The data contract class, `ServiceInfo` will have one property named `ServiceName`. The service contract, `ISimpleService` is an interface class, which will have one function, `GetServiceInfo`:

```
namespace Recipe1_SimpleService
{
  [DataContract]
  public class ServiceInfo
  {
    [DataMember]
    public string ServiceName { get; set; }


  }

  // NOTE: You can use the "Rename" command on the "Refactor" menu
  //   to change the interface name "ISimpleService" in both code and
  //   config file together.

  [ServiceContract]
  public interface ISimpleService
  {
    [OperationContract]
    string GetServiceInfo();
  }
}
```

3. Now open the `SimpleService.svc.cs` file and add the `public` function `GetServiceInfo`. This method just returns a string `"Simple Service Demo"` when the service is called from the client:

```
public class SimpleService : ISimpleService
{
  public string GetServiceInfo()
  {
    return "Simple Service Demo";
  }
}
```

4. Press *F5*, and then build and run the service. You should be presented with a **WCF Test Client**, which is an easy way to test the service. Select the **ISimpleService** and then click on **GetServiceInfo** and you will get an option to **Invoke**. When you invoke the service method you should see the request and response in XML formats, as shown in the following screenshot:

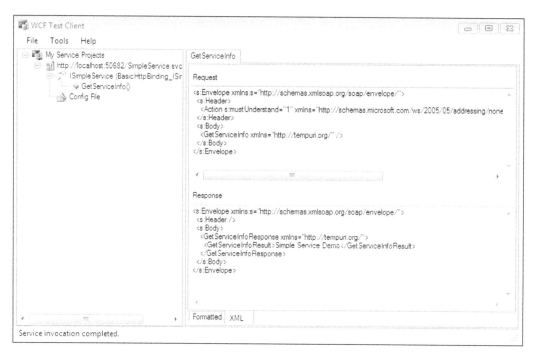

5. We just created a simple WCF service, which can be hosted in the web server environment or we can run it in the localhost so we can test the service with a client application.

6. Now let's build a client Phone 7 application to consume this service. Open the new project and create a Phone 7 Application. Name it `Recipe1_SimpleServiceClient`.

7. Right-click on the **References** folder and add **Service Reference** to the project. Type in the localhost service URI into the address textbox and click on **Go**. This will create all the proxy classes in the client application to help make calls to the WCF Service. Also, type the **Reference** name as `SimpleServiceReference`. After adding the service, the project should look like the following screenshot:

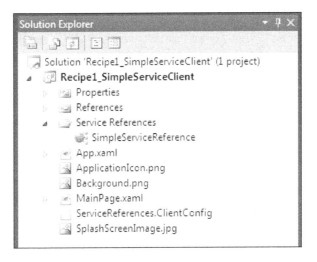

8. Open the `MainPage.xaml` file; let's add a button and a **textblock** control to display the return string from the service.

```
<!--TitlePanel contains the name of the application and page
  title-->
<StackPanel x:Name="TitlePanel" Grid.Row="0" Margin="12,17,0,28">
  <TextBlock x:Name="ApplicationTitle" Text="MY APPLICATION"
    Style="{StaticResource PhoneTextNormalStyle}"/>

  <TextBlock x:Name="PageTitle" Text="Simple Service" Margin="9,-
    7,0,0" Style="{StaticResource PhoneTextTitle1Style}"/>
</StackPanel>

<!--ContentPanel - place additional content here-->
<Grid x:Name="ContentPanel" Grid.Row="1" Margin="12,0,12,0">

  <Button Content="Call Service" Height="72"
    HorizontalAlignment="Left" Margin="37,63,0,0" Name="button1"
    VerticalAlignment="Top" Width="379" Click="button1_Click" />
  <TextBlock Height="59" HorizontalAlignment="Left"
    Margin="51,194,0,0" Name="textBlock1" Text="Results"
    VerticalAlignment="Top" Width="365" />

</Grid>
```

9. Open the `MainPage.xaml.cs` file and add the `using` declarative to the service reference at the beginning of the file:

```
using Recipe1_SimpleServiceClient.SimpleServiceReference;
```

10. Add an instance of the context object for `SimpleServiceClient` in the `MainPage` class, as follows:

```
public partial class MainPage : PhoneApplicationPage
{
  // Constructor
  SimpleServiceClient ssc;
  public MainPage()
```

11. Add an `EventHandler` to catch the `GetServiceInfoCompleted` event as shown in the following code:

```
public MainPage()
{
  InitializeComponent();

  ssc = new SimpleServiceClient();

  ssc.GetServiceInfoCompleted += new
    EventHandler<GetServiceInfoCompletedEventArgs>
    (ssc_GetServiceInfoCompleted);

}

void ssc_GetServiceInfoCompleted(object sender,
  GetServiceInfoCompletedEventArgs e)
{
  if (e.Result != null)
  {
    textBlock1.Text = e.Result.ToString();
  }
}
```

12. Now add the button click event and call the `GetServiceInfoAsync` method:

```
private void button1_Click(object sender, RoutedEventArgs e)
{
  ssc.GetServiceInfoAsync();
}
```

13. Press *F5* , and when you click on the **Call Service** button you should get the service info string from the WCF service:

How it works...

In this recipe, we created a simple service to understand what it takes to create the service and consume it using a Phone 7 client.

The `ISimpleService` file defines the `DataContract` and `ServiceContract`. Based on this, the client can access the `Member` class and property. `ServiceContract` is the method available for the client's consumption.

When the service is added to the client application, a method that is defined as `ServiceContract`, such as `GetServiceInfo` is visible and can be invoked to get the results.

There's more...

This recipe is a simple demonstration of a service model. In the next couple of recipes we will dive deeper into topics such as connecting to a database and using the Entity Framework to create all the proxy classes.

See also

Check the recipe *Using LINQ to SQL for creating the service* in this chapter.

Building a service layer using WCF

In the last recipe, we learned how to call a simple WCF service from the client application. In this recipe let's create a `MyTasks` Service.

Getting ready

Create a new project using the WCF service template and follow the same steps as in the recipe *Writing and consuming a simple web service* to create the service.

How to do it...

In this recipe, we will first create the WCF service and then build the Data Contract and Service Contract. In the Data Contract, we will add all the Data members; in the Service Contract we will return a collection class. Once the service is built successfully, we create the Phone Client application to call the service when searching for a task name.

1. Right-click on the project and click on **Add new item**. Select the **WCF service template** and name it `MyTaskService.svc`.

2. Open the `IMyTaskService.cs` file and add the following code for class `MyTask` and `IMyTaskService`:

```
namespace Recipe2_MyTasksService
{
  [DataContract]
  public class MyTask
  {
    [DataMember]
    public string Name { get; set; }
    [DataMember]
    public string Notes { get; set; }
    [DataMember]
    public string Priority { get; set; }
    [DataMember]
    public DateTime DateDue { get; set; }
    [DataMember]
    public DateTime DateCreated { get; set; }
  }

  [ServiceContract]
  public interface IMyTaskService
  {
    [OperationContract]
    List<string> GetMyTaskList();

    [OperationContract]
    MyTask GetMyTask(string Name);
  }
}
```

3. Now let's add a collection class for `MyTask`. Right-click on the project and add a new class. Name this class `MyTasks.cs`. Open the file and add the following code:

```
namespace Recipe2_MyTasksService
{
  public class MyTasks : List<MyTask>
  {
    public MyTasks()
    {
      LoadSampleTasks();
    }

    public List<string> GetMyTaskList()
    {
      var lst = this.Select(t => new { t.Name });

      return lst as List<string>;
    }

    public MyTask GetMyTask(string name)
    {
      return this.Where(t => t.Name == name).First();
    }

    public void LoadSampleTasks()
    {
      MyTask myTask = new MyTask()
      {
        Name = "Task Name 1",
        Notes = "Task Note 1",
        Priority = "Low",
        DateDue = new DateTime(2011, 9, 1),
        DateCreated = DateTime.Now
      };
      this.Add(myTask);

      myTask = new MyTask()
      {
        Name = "Task Name 2",
        Notes = "Task Note 2",
        Priority = "Medium",
        DateDue = new DateTime(2011, 10, 1),
        DateCreated = DateTime.Now
      };
```

```
        this.Add(myTask);

        myTask = new MyTask()
        {
          Name = "Task Name 3",
          Notes = "Task Note 3",
          Priority = "High",
          DateDue = new DateTime(2011, 11, 1),
          DateCreated = DateTime.Now
        };
        this.Add(myTask);
      }
    }
  }
```

4. Open the `MyTaskService.svc.cs` file and add two public methods
    `GetMyTaskList` and `GetMyTask`. `GetMyTaskList` returns the list of tasks and
    `GetMyTask` returns the name of the task, as follows:

```
namespace Recipe2_MyTasksService
{
  public class MyTaskService : IMyTaskService
  {
    public List<string> GetMyTaskList()
    {
      MyTasks mytaskList = new MyTasks();

      return mytaskList.GetMyTaskList();
    }

    public MyTask GetMyTask(string name)
    {
      MyTasks mytaskList = new MyTasks();

      return mytaskList.GetMyTask(name);
    }
  }
}
```

5. Press *F5* and you should see the **WCF Test Client** as shown in the following
    screenshot. Click on the **IMyTaskService** item to see the two methods. You can easily
    test the service here by passing a task name to get the priority.

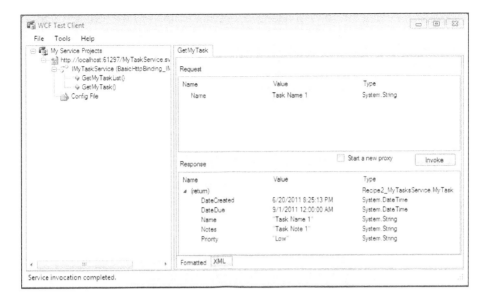

6. Now let's create a new project to consume the service we created. Name the project `Recipe2_MyTaskClient`. Add the service reference similar to the last recipe and type the namespace `MyTaskServiceReference`.

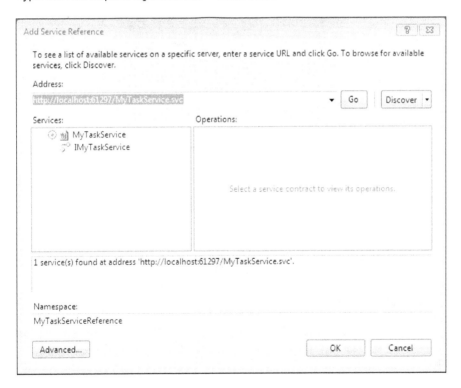

7. Now after adding the code similar to last recipe for the context object, run the application. You should see the following results when you type in the name under **Task Name** and click on **Get the Priority**.

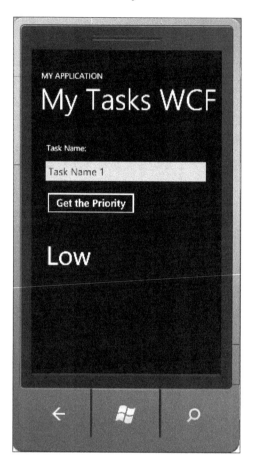

How it works...

In this recipe, we created a class to store all the information for MyTask.

Using the service model, we built service classes to expose the members. We then added the collection class to return MyTask as a list object to the Phone Client Application.

There's more...

In this recipe, we didn't use SQL Server for storing our data to keep it simple to understand. In the next recipe, we will use SQL Server as the backend database to store our tasks.

See also

Check the next recipe, which deals with the ADO.NET Entity Framework. Also, check the recipe *Using LINQ to SQL for creating the service*.

WCF using ADO.NET Entity Framework

In this recipe, let's use the SQL Server database as the backend. We will create the `MyTask` table in the SQL Server Express database.

Getting ready

For this recipe, let's create a WCF service project similar to the last recipe. Let's call this project `Recipe3_WCFSQLService`.

How to do it...

In this recipe, we will create the WCF Service project with SQL Server as the backend database. We use the ADO.NET Entity Framework to create all the entity objects, and then we add the methods to return the results to the client application.

1. In this recipe, we will add SQL Server Express database to the project. Name it `MyTasks.mdf`.

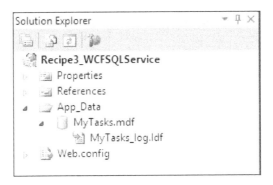

2. Double-click the database to open it and then right-click on **Tables** to add a new table. Call this table `MyTask` and add the columns as shown in the following screenshot:

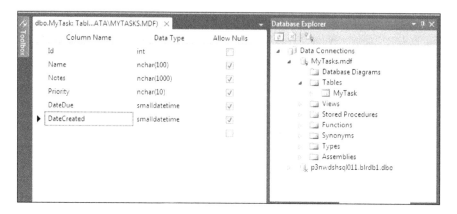

3. After the table is created, add a couple of test records using insert statements; or you can directly enter them in the result grid.

4. Now using the graphical view build a query by selecting all the columns from the table **MyTask**. When you run the query you should see two test rows from the table and this is illustrated in the next screenshot:

5. Now let's use the ADO.NET Entity Data Model to generate proxy classes. Right-click the project and select **Add New item**. Select **ADO.NET Entity Data Model** from the dialog box:

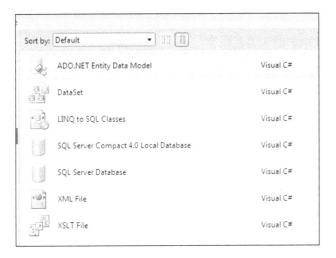

6. You are given a choice to create the model using either **Generate from database** or **Empty model**. Select the **Generate from Database** icon and click on **Next**. This will take you to another dialog box with a list of objects in the database.

7. Next select the database objects. Select the **Tables** folder and check the **MyTask (dbo)** checkbox. Type `MyTaskModel` under **Model Namespace**. Click on the **Finish** button, as shown in the following screenshot:

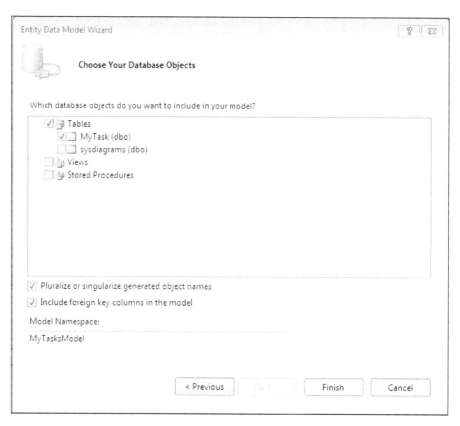

8. Once complete, the `MyTask.edmx` file is added to the project. When you open this file you should see the model as shown in the following screenshot:

9. Now add a new item and select the **WCF Service** template. Name the file
   MyTaskService.svc, as shown in the following screenshot. When created, it adds
   IMyTaskService and MyTaskService.svc files.

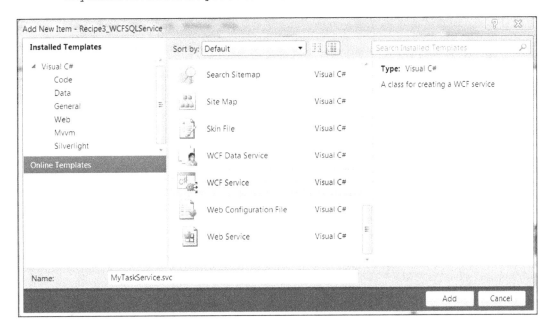

10. Open the IMyTaskService.cs file and add a ServiceContract:

```
[ServiceContract]
public interface IMyTaskService
{
  [OperationContract]
  MyTask GetTask(int value);
}
```

11. Now open the MyTaskService.svc file and implement the GetTask function:

```
public MyTask GetTask(int value)
{
  MyTasksEntities _ctx = new MyTasksEntities();

  return _ctx.MyTasks.Where(c=>c.Id == value).Single();
}
```

12. Now press *F5* and run the project.

13. Once the service is built, let's build the client application. Create a new Phone 7
    Application and name it Recipe3_WcfSqlClient.

14. Right-click on **Service References** in the project and select **Add Service Reference**. Copy the service address into **Address** or click on the down arrow mark in the **Address** dropdown. This is shown in the following screenshot:

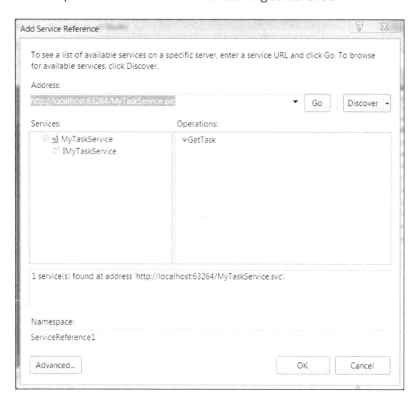

15. Open the `MainPage.xaml` file and change the `ApplicationTitle` and `PageTitle` properties in the `TextBlock` controls:

```
<!--TitlePanel contains the name of the application and page
   title-->
<StackPanel x:Name="TitlePanel" Grid.Row="0" Margin="12,17,0,28">

   <TextBlock x:Name="ApplicationTitle" Text="MY RECIPES"
      Style="{StaticResource PhoneTextNormalStyle}"/>

   <TextBlock x:Name="PageTitle" Text="WCF SQL EF" Margin="9,-
      7,0,0" Style="{StaticResource PhoneTextTitle1Style}"/>

</StackPanel>
```

16. Add a textbox, to search for the task id, and a button to click in the first content grid:

```
<!--ContentPanel - place additional content here-->
<Grid x:Name="ContentPanel" Grid.Row="1" Margin="12,0">
  <TextBox Height="72" HorizontalAlignment="Left"
    Margin="0,52,0,0" Name="textBox1" Text=""
    VerticalAlignment="Top" Width="460" />
  <TextBlock Height="30" HorizontalAlignment="Left"
    Margin="14,32,0,0" Name="textBlock1" Text="Task Id:"
    VerticalAlignment="Top" />
  <Button Content="Get Task Details" Height="72"
    HorizontalAlignment="Left" Margin="0,116,0,0" Name="button1"
    VerticalAlignment="Top" Width="243" Click="button1_Click" />
</Grid>
```

17. Now add another Grid with the name `ContentPanel2`. Add four `RowDefintions` and two `ColumnDefinitions`. Add four `TextBlock` controls to display the task details:

```
<!--ContentPanel - place additional content here-->
<Grid x:Name="ContentPanel2" Margin="12,217,12,-13" Grid.Row="1">
  <Grid.RowDefinitions>
    <RowDefinition Height="50"/>
    <RowDefinition Height="50"/>
    <RowDefinition Height="50"/>
    <RowDefinition Height="50"/>
  </Grid.RowDefinitions>

  <Grid.ColumnDefinitions>
    <ColumnDefinition Width="100" />
    <ColumnDefinition Width="300" />
  </Grid.ColumnDefinitions>

  <TextBlock Grid.Row="0" Grid.Column="0" Text="Name:" />

  <TextBlock Grid.Row="0" Grid.Column="1" Text="{Binding Name}"
    FontWeight="Bold" Foreground="OrangeRed"/>

  <TextBlock Grid.Row="1" Grid.Column="0" Text="DateDue:" />

  <TextBlock Grid.Row="1" Grid.Column="1" Text="
    {Binding DateDue}" />

  <TextBlock Grid.Row="2" Grid.Column="0" Text="Priority:" />
  <TextBlock Grid.Row="2" Grid.Column="1" Text="{Binding
    Priority}"  Foreground="Yellow"/>
```

```
  <TextBlock Grid.Row="3" Grid.Column="0" Text="Notes:" />

  <TextBlock Grid.Row="3" Grid.Column="1" Text="
    {Binding Notes}" />

</Grid>
```

18. Open the `MainPage.xaml.cs` file, and add a reference to the WCF service we referenced at the top of the page:

    ```
    using Recipe3_WcfSqlService.ServiceReference1;
    ```

19. Declare an object to context class `MyTaskServiceClient` before the `MainPage` constructor:

    ```
    public partial class MainPage : PhoneApplicationPage
    {
      MyTaskServiceClient _context;
      // Constructor
      public MainPage()
      {
    ..
    ```

20. Next, initialize the context object and add the event handler delegate as follows:

    ```
    public MainPage()
    {
      InitializeComponent();
      _context = new MyTaskServiceClient();
      _context.GetTaskCompleted += new
        EventHandler<GetTaskCompletedEventArgs>(GetTaskCompleted);
    }

    void GetTaskCompleted(object sender, GetTaskCompletedEventArgs e)
    {
      if (e.Result != null)
      {
        this.DataContext = e.Result;
      }
    }
    ```

21. Add the button click event method that will call the `GetTaskAsync` method with `id` as the parameter:

    ```
    private void button1_Click(object sender, RoutedEventArgs e)
    {
      if(!String.IsNullOrEmpty(textBox1.Text))
        _context.GetTaskAsync(int.Parse(textBox1.Text));
    }
    ```

22. Press *F5*, type in a **Task Id** and click the **Get Task Details** button. You should see the result as shown in the following screenshot:

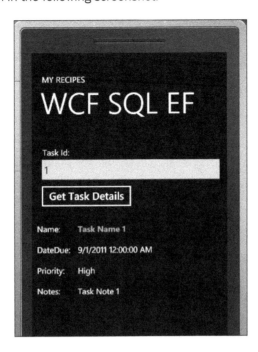

How it works...

All the main functionalities in this recipe are added by the Entity Framework model. Open the `MyTask.designer.cs` file and you can see the code generated in two categories: Context and other Entities.

Context class takes care of connecting to the backend database and Entities creates the `MyTask` class out of the `MyTask` table with all the columns as properties.

There's more...

In this recipe, we demonstrated how to get the results and display them. The Entity Framework has all the functionalities to update and delete as well. By updating the entity context we can easily update the backend database.

See also

In the next recipe, we will learn how to implement similar functionalities to those in this recipe, but by using LINQ to SQL.

Using LINQ to SQL for creating the service

LINQ to SQL is the family of LINQ technologies targeting relational databases where data is mapped as objects. LINQ to SQL provides the fastest way to create an interface to the backend. The only disadvantage is it can only map one level of relationship. So, if you need deeper relationship management, the Entity Framework is the way to go. Some of the features of LINQ to SQL are as follows:

- Translates LINQ expression to **T-SQL** (**Transact-SQL**)
- Provides an easy way to query objects instead of SQL statements
- Has the ability to create databases and tables in the database
- Provides a way to query the database using regular T-SQL statements

In this recipe, let's build the `MyTask` service like the preceding recipe, but instead of using the Entity Framework we will use LINQ to SQL classes.

Getting ready

Open the Visual Studio and create a new project using the **WCF Service Application template** and name it `Recipe4_LINQToSQL` under the CH7 folder. Right-click on **App_Data** and select **Add new item**. Navigate to the preceding recipe's **App_Data** folder and select the `MyTask.mdf` file. We will use the same database and the `MyTask` table.

How to do it...

For this recipe, we will again be creating the service application, but this time we will use LINQ to SQL to create the entity objects.

1. Delete `IService1.cs` and `Service1.svc` from the project.
2. Right-click on the project and **Add new item**. Select the **LINQ to SQL Classes** template and name it `MyTaskDataModel`, as shown in the following screenshot. When you click on `Add`, you should see the `MyTaskDataModel.dbml` file in your project.

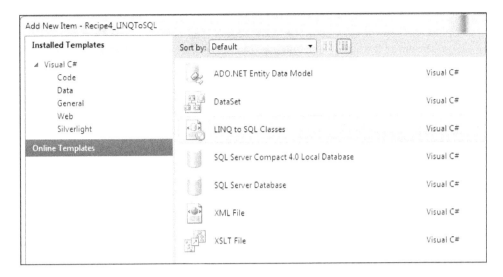

3. Now let's add another new item to the project. Select **WCF Service** as the file template. Name this file `MyTaskService.svc`.

4. Open the `MyTaskService.cs` file and add a `get` function to return the `MyTask` class:

```
[ServiceContract]
public interface IMyTaskService
{
  [OperationContract]
  MyTask GetTask(int value);
}
```

5. Now, open the `MyTaskService.svc.cs` file and let's add the details for the `GetTask` function. In this method, we shall create a data context object and use the LINQ syntax for getting the task by `Id`:

```
public class MyTaskService : IMyTaskService
{
  public MyTask GetTask(int value)
  {
    MyTaskDataModelDataContext ctx = new
      MyTaskDataModelDataContext();

    return ctx.MyTasks.Where(c => c.Id == value).Single();
  }
}
```

6. Right-click on `MyTaskService.svc` and set it as start page. Now press *F5* to run. You should see the service in the **WCF Test Client**. Select the **GetTask** request and type a **value** of **2** and click on **Invoke.** You should see the following screenshot:

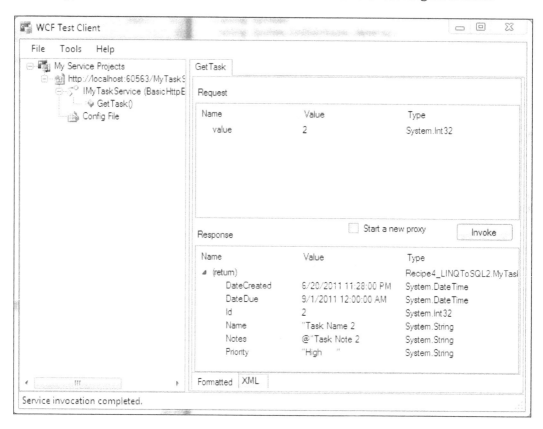

7. Now let's create a client application to consume this data service exactly like the preceding recipe. Create a new Phone 7 Application and name it `Recipe4_LINQToSQLClient`.

8. **Add Service Reference**; you will be prompted by a dialog box like shown in the following screenshot:

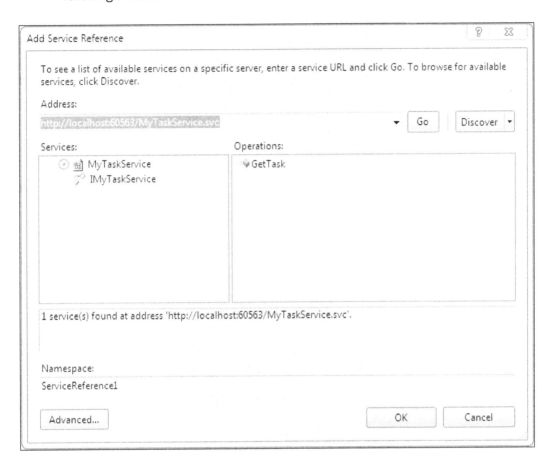

9. Add the context object and the event handler similar to steps 18, 19, and 20 of the previous recipe.

10. Press *F5*. You should get the main page as shown in the following screenshot. When you type the **Task Id** and click on **Get Task Details** you should get the details of the task.

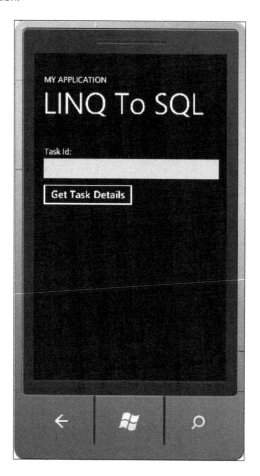

How it works...

LINQ to SQL creates the .dbml file. This file is the proxy file generated by LINQ with the data context object. This file has the class definition for the table, relationships, and properties.

If you open the file MyTaskDataModel.designer.cs, then you can see the following data context class. This class connects to the database using a connection string that is saved in the config file.

```
public partial class MyTaskDataModelDataContext :
  System.Data.Linq.DataContext
{
```

```
private static System.Data.Linq.Mapping.MappingSource
  mappingSource = new AttributeMappingSource();

#region Extensibility Method Definitions
partial void OnCreated();
#endregion

public MyTaskDataModelDataContext() :
  base(global::System.Configuration.ConfigurationManager.
  ConnectionStrings["MyTasksConnectionString"].ConnectionString,
  mappingSource)
{

  OnCreated();
}
```

We can also see how all the records in the `MyTask` table are returned in the following code:

```
public System.Data.Linq.Table<MyTask> MyTasks
{
  get
  {
    return this.GetTable<MyTask>();
  }
}
```

LINQ to SQL also creates the `MyTask` class with all the table columns as properties. LINQ to SQL supports many types of attributes such as `TableAttribute`, `ColumnAttribute`, `AssociationAttribute`, `FunctionAttribute`, table, and so on. We can see the different values of `ColumnAttribute` in this file.

There's more...

In this sample, we just created a simple recipe that invokes a `GetTask` method to get a specific task row. Using the `DataContext` class, we can also update and delete records in the table.

See also

In an earlier recipe, *WCF using ADO.NET Entity Framework*, we covered how to use the Entity Framework. The EF is considered more robust than LINQ to SQL. So, for databases with deeper relationships and for more scalability use the Entity Framework.

8
Model View ViewModel

In this chapter, we will cover:

- ► Simple MVVM applications
- ► Using MVVM Light Toolkit
- ► Updating the MVVM application

Introduction

Model View ViewModel (**MVVM**) is a UI software design pattern similar to **Model View Controller** (**MVC**). MVVM allows separation of concerns and makes the application very flexible and easy to maintain. Designers can work independently with the user interface while developers work on the model and the back-end coding.

Applications built on the MVVM pattern should have the following three distinctive layers:

1. **View**: This is the front-end or user interface code such as XAML with very little or no code-behind.

2. **ViewModel**: This is the code between View and Model. ViewModel acts as a bridge between the user interface and the model. This layer can have all the presentation layer code that connects to the model. This makes it easy to test the user interface functionality of the application.

3. **Model**: This layer contains the classes that represent data or entities. This can include business logic and data access layers.

MVVM also will have notification mechanism to send a message to the client whenever the model data changes. This is illustrated in the following diagram:

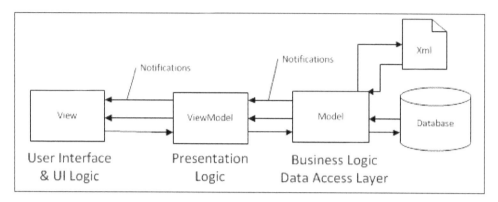

Multiple ideas of Views can be tested without changing the code that connects to the data. Furthermore, unit testing can be performed on the ViewModel side without any interfaces. This chapter looks into different aspects of the MVVM pattern using simple recipes to complex ones. For more information on this pattern check this article:

```
http://msdn.microsoft.com/en-us/magazine/dd419663.aspx
```

Simple MVVM application

In this recipe, we will cover the basic principles of MVVM by creating a simple Phone 7 application with ViewModel and sample data.

Getting ready

Let's create a new Phone 7 Project with a project name `Recipe1_SimpleMVVM` and a solution name `Ch8_Recipes`.

How to do it...

Here we will create a simple user interface with a list box to display text in two `TextBlock` controls. Then, we will add the `ViewModel` class, which returns data from the sample data.

1. Open `MainPage.xaml` and change the `ApplicationTitle` and `PageTitle`:

    ```xml
    <StackPanel x:Name="TitlePanel" Grid.Row="0" Margin="12,17,0,28">
      <TextBlock x:Name="ApplicationTitle" Text="Data Recipes"
        Style="{StaticResource PhoneTextNormalStyle}"/>
      <TextBlock x:Name="PageTitle" Text="Simple MVVM" Margin="9,-
        7,0,0" Style="{StaticResource PhoneTextTitle1Style}"/>
    </StackPanel>
    ```

2. Add two `TextBlock` controls as shown in the following code snippet. We will be using one for `TaskName` and the other for `TaskNotes`:

```
<Grid x:Name="ContentPanel" Grid.Row="1" Margin="12,0,12,0">
  <ListBox x:Name="MainListBox" Margin="0,0,-12,0"
    ItemsSource="{Binding Items}">
  <ListBox.ItemTemplate>
    <DataTemplate>
      <StackPanel Margin="0,0,0,17" Width="432">
        <TextBlock Text="{Binding TaskName}" TextWrapping="Wrap"
          Style="{StaticResource PhoneTextExtraLargeStyle}"/>
        <TextBlock Text="{Binding TaskNotes}"
          TextWrapping="Wrap" Margin="12,-6,12,0"
          Style="{StaticResource PhoneTextSubtleStyle}"/>
      </StackPanel>
    </DataTemplate>
  </ListBox.ItemTemplate>
  </ListBox>
</Grid>
```

3. Press *F5* and run it to make sure there are no errors.

4. Now right-click on the **Project** folder and add a new folder with the name `ViewModel`.

5. Right-click on the folder `ViewModel` and add a new class called `ViewModelBase`, which is inherited from `INotifyPropertyChanged`. Here we will add declarations for events such as `PropertyChangedEventHandler` and a method named `NotifyPropertyChanged`.

```
public class ViewModelBase : INotifyPropertyChanged
{
  public event PropertyChangedEventHandler PropertyChanged;

  public void NotifyPropertyChanged(String propertyName)
  {
    if (null != PropertyChanged)
    {
      PropertyChanged(this, new
        PropertyChangedEventArgs(propertyName));
    }
  }
}
```

6. Add a new class and name it `MyTaskItemViewModel.cs` and then add the following code, which has the class `MyTaskItemViewModel` derived from `ViewModelBase` and has properties `TaskName` and `TaskNotes`:

```csharp
namespace Recipe1_SimpleMVVM.ViewModel
{
  public class MyTaskItemViewModel : ViewModelBase
  {
    private string _taskName;
    public string TaskName
    {
      get
      {
        return _taskName;
      }
      set
      {
        _taskName = value;
        NotifyPropertyChanged("TaskName");
      }
    }
    private string _taskNotes;
    public string TaskNotes
    {
      get
      {
        return _taskNotes;
      }
      set
      {
        _taskNotes = value;
        NotifyPropertyChanged("TaskNotes");
      }
    }

  }
}
```

7. Right-click on `ViewModel` again and add a new class with the name `MyTaskViewModel.cs`. Open the file and add the following references at the start:

```csharp
using System.ComponentModel;
using System.Collections.ObjectModel;
```

8. Now add the code for class `MyTaskViewModel` inheriting from `ViewModelBase`. Here we have the `ObservableCollection` property for `Items` and a Boolean property for `IsDataLoaded`. Then, we have the method `LoadData`, which will add the sample to the `Items` collection:

```
namespace Recipe1_SimpleMVVM.ViewModel
{
  public class MyTaskViewModel : ViewModelBase
  {

    public MyTaskViewModel()
    {
      // Insert code required on object creation below this point.
      this.Items = new ObservableCollection
        <MyTaskItemViewModel>();
    }

    /// <summary>
    /// A collection for ItemViewModel objects.
    /// </summary>
    public ObservableCollection<MyTaskItemViewModel>
      Items { get; private set; }

    public bool IsDataLoaded
    {
      get;
      private set;
    }

    /// <summary>
    /// Creates and adds a few MyTaskItemViewModel objects
    ///   into the Items collection.
    /// </summary>
    public void LoadData()
    {
      // Sample data; replace with real data
      this.Items.Add(new MyTaskItemViewModel() { TaskName
        = "Task 1", TaskNotes = "Task Notes 1" });
      this.Items.Add(new MyTaskItemViewModel() { TaskName
        = "Task 2", TaskNotes = "Task Notes 2" });
      this.Items.Add(new MyTaskItemViewModel() { TaskName
        = "Task 3", TaskNotes = "Task Notes 3" });
      this.IsDataLoaded = true;
    }

  }

}
```

9. Now open the `App.xaml.cs` file and add the `ViewModel` global property as shown in the following code snippet:

```
public partial class App : Application
{
  private static ViewModel.MyTaskViewModel viewModel = null;
  /// <summary>
  /// A static ViewModel used by the views to bind against.
  /// </summary>
  /// <returns>The MyTaskViewModel object.</returns>
  public static ViewModel.MyTaskViewModel ViewModel
  {
    get
    {
      // Delay creation of the view model until necessary
      if (viewModel == null)
        viewModel = new ViewModel.MyTaskViewModel();

      return viewModel;
    }
  }
}
```

10. Now let's add the code in the `MainPage.xaml.cs` file to load the data into `DataContext` and its items:

```
public partial class MainPage : PhoneApplicationPage
{
  // Constructor
  public MainPage()
  {
    InitializeComponent();
    DataContext = App.ViewModel;
    this.Loaded += new  RoutedEventHandler(MainPage_Loaded);
  }

  // Load data for the ViewModel Items
  private void MainPage_Loaded(object sender, RoutedEventArgs e)
  {
    if (!App.ViewModel.IsDataLoaded)
    {
      App.ViewModel.LoadData();
    }
  }
}
```

11. Press *F5* and run to see the results as shown in the following screenshot:

How it works...

In this recipe, we added two classes `MyTaskItemViewModel.cs` and `MyTaskViewModel.cs`. The class `MyTaskItemViewModel` defines the list of task line items that we are going to store. Here we are just defining two properties for simplicity, `TaskName` and `TaskNotes`. We created a `ViewModelBase` class which is inherited from `INotifyPropertyChanged` to make this class bindable to the UI. We added the `NotfiyPropertyChanged` method and called it when setting each property.

In the `MyTaskViewModel` class, we initialized the `MyTaskItemViewModel` as `ObservableCollection`. We added a method `LoadData()` to load the sample data into the `Items` collection. In the `app.xaml.cs` file, we defined the static global property for creating the `MyTaskViewModel` class.

Finally, we initialized the `App.ViewModel` object to the `DataContext` object so that when the page is loaded, an event is fired to load the test data.

There's more...

In this recipe, we just learned a simple MVVM recipe without much complexity. To make it easy to implement there are many MVVM toolkits and templates available. In the next recipe, we will explore how we can make it easy by using a project template that comes with Visual Studio.

How to use the project template

In the last recipe, we understood the different steps involved in creating a simple MVVM recipe. We can create the project with all the different layers using the **Windows Phone Databound Application project** template.

1. Open a new project and pick the project template named **Windows Phone Databound Application** and name it `Recipe2_DataboundApp`.

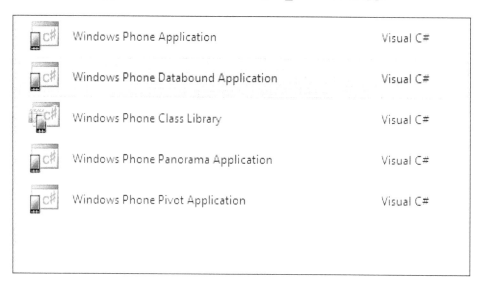

2. You should see the following file structure created by the project template by default. This is exactly similar to what we learned in the preceding recipe.

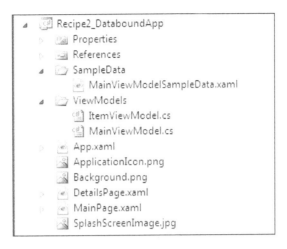

3. Press *F5* and run it. You should see the following results without adding any line of code.

See also

Check the next recipe in this chapter to further understand how MVVM can be easily adapted to your applications to make it easy to test and maintain. At the time of writing this book, Visual Studio Express 2010 for Windows Phone development doesn't support any toolkit for creating MVVM, so we are going to explore the toolkit called MVVM Light Toolkit, which will help us create all the plumbing required for typical MVVM-patterned applications.

Using MVVM Light Toolkit

Sometimes, MVVM can have too many layers and become complex. So to avoid this we can use frameworks or toolkits, which will make it easy to start. There were many toolkits available at the time of writing this book. A simple and popular toolkit is **MVVM Light Toolkit**, which helps us build MVVM quickly and contains only the essential components. In this recipe let's build a sample using this toolkit.

Getting ready

Before we start creating a recipe, let's download the MVVM Light Toolkit from the following URL: `http://mvvmlight.codeplex.com/`. Download the latest version and save it to your local folder. If you are using Vista or Windows 7, you should unblock the files by right-clicking and selecting **Properties**. Then, click on the **Unblock** button in the **General** tab at the bottom. Check the website for more instructions on how to manually install the software. After successfully installing it, open the new project and you should see the **MvvmLight (WP7)** template as shown in the following screenshot:

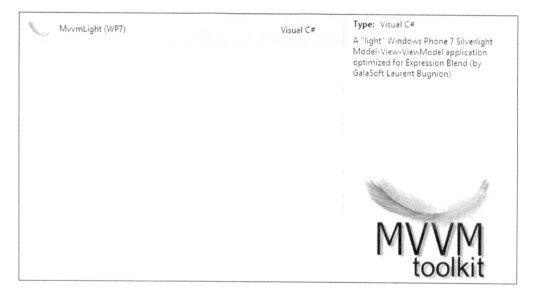

How to do it...

In the following steps we will create an application using the **MvvmLight** project template to display MyTasks.

1. Open the new project and select the **MvvmLight (WP7)** project template and name the project Recipe3_MvvmLight. When you click on **OK**, you should see the following project structure:

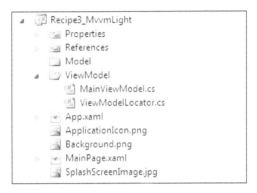

2. Make sure two reference files GalaSoft.MvvmLight.Extras.WP7 and GalaSoft.MvvmLight.WP7 exist in the References folder.

3. Press *F5* and you should see the **Welcome to MVVM Light** message as shown in the following screenshot:

4. Under the project folder, right-click on the reference folder and add a reference to the assembly `System.Runtime.Serialization`.

5. Now add the `MyTask.cs` file to the `Model` folder. Open the `MyTask.cs` file and add the following two `using` statements.

```
using System.ComponentModel;
using System.Runtime.Serialization;
```

6. Now, let's inherit `MyTask` from the `INotifyPropertyChanged` class to support direct binding to the UI. Then, we call the `NotifyPropertyChanged` method for each property in the set property. Whenever the property is set with a value, a message is triggered to the View to refresh the UI.

```
namespace Recipe3_MvvmLightMyTasks.Model
{
  [DataContract()]
  public class MyTask : INotifyPropertyChanged
  {
    private string _name;
    private string _notes;
    private string _priority;
    private DateTime _dateDue;
    private DateTime _dateCreated;

    [DataMemberAttribute()]
    public string Name
    {
      get
      {
        return _name;
      }
      set
      {
        _name = value;
        NotifyPropertyChanged("Name");
      }
    }

    [DataMemberAttribute()]
    public string Notes
    {
      get
      {
        return _notes;
      }
      set
```

```
    {
      _notes = value;
      NotifyPropertyChanged("Notes");
    }
  }

  [DataMemberAttribute()]
  public string Priority
  {
    get
    {
      return _priority;
    }
    set
    {
      _priority = value;
      NotifyPropertyChanged("Priority");
    }
  }

  [DataMemberAttribute()]
  public DateTime DateDue
  {
    get
    {
      return _dateDue;
    }
    set
    {
      _dateDue = value;
      NotifyPropertyChanged("DateDue");
    }
  }

  [DataMemberAttribute()]
  public DateTime DateCreated
  {
    get
    {
      return _dateCreated;
    }
    set
    {
      _dateCreated = value;
```

```
            NotifyPropertyChanged("DateCreated");
          }
        }

        public event PropertyChangedEventHandler PropertyChanged;
        private void NotifyPropertyChanged(string propertyName)
        {
          if (null != PropertyChanged)
            PropertyChanged(this, new
              PropertyChangedEventArgs(propertyName));

        }
      }
    }
```

7. Right-click on the **ViewModel** folder and add a new item. Pick the **MvvmViewModel** template and name it `MyTaskViewModel.cs`.

8. Add the following `using` statement at the start of the file:

```
using Recipe3_MvvmLightMyTasks.Model;
using System.Collections.ObjectModel;
```

9. Let's add the code to load the sample tasks. In this recipe, we will make it simple to load the sample data. `MyTaskViewModel` is inherited from the `ViewModelBase` class, which is part of MVVM Light SDK:

```
public class MyTaskViewModel : ViewModelBase
{
  public string ApplicationTitle
  {
    get
    {
      return "MVVM Recipes";
    }
  }

  public string PageName
  {
    get
    {
      return "MyTasks View";
    }
  }

  public MyTaskViewModel()
  {
```

```
    LoadSampleTasks();
  }

  private ObservableCollection<MyTask> myTasks;
  public ObservableCollection<MyTask> MyTasks
  {
    get
    {
      return myTasks;
    }
  }

  public void LoadSampleTasks()
  {
    myTasks = new ObservableCollection<MyTask>()
    {
    new MyTask() {Name = "Task 1", Notes= "Task 1 Notes", Priority
      = "High", DateDue = System.DateTime.Parse("10/01/2011")
      ,DateCreated = System.DateTime.Now},
    new MyTask() {Name = "Task 2", Notes= "Task 2 Notes",
      Priority = "Medium", DateDue =
      System.DateTime.Parse("11/15/2011"),
      DateCreated = System.DateTime.Now},
    new MyTask() {Name = "Task 3", Notes= "Task 3 Notes",
      Priority = "Low", DateDue =
      System.DateTime.Parse("12/30/2011"),DateCreated =
      System.DateTime.Now}
    };
  }
}
```

10. Now let's create another folder called `View` in the project and add a new class file called `MyTaksView` using the `MvvmView` template. When you are done adding the page, you should see a view similar to that of a `MainPage`.

11. Now add a `TextBlock` control with the `MouseLeftButtonDown` event property set to the `TextBlock_MouseLeftButtonDown` event method as illustrated in the following code snippet:

```
<Grid x:Name="ContentGrid" Grid.Row="1">
  <TextBlock Text="{Binding NavLinkName}"
    Style="{StaticResource PhoneTextNormalStyle}"
    HorizontalAlignment="Center"
    VerticalAlignment="Center"
    FontSize="40"
    MouseLeftButtonDown="TextBlock_MouseLeftButtonDown"/>
</Grid>
```

12. Right-click on `TextBlock_MouseLeftButtonDown` and navigate to the code-behind. Add the navigation code so that when you click you should navigate to the `MyTaskView` page:

```
private void TextBlock_MouseLeftButtonDown(object sender,
  System.Windows.Input.MouseButtonEventArgs e)
{
  NavigationService.Navigate(new
    Uri("/View/MyTaskView.xaml",UriKind.Relative));
}
```

13. Rename the `Welcome` property to `NavLinkName`, which displays the navigation `TextBlock` text in the main page instead of the welcome message as displayed in step 3:

```
public string NavLinkName
{
  get
  {
    return "View MyTasks List";
  }
}
```

14. Open the `MyTaskView.xaml` file and add a list control as shown in the following code snippet. For simplicity we are going to use the inline styling to color code which is not recommend as a best practice. In the next recipe you will see how to use the resources to define the styles for controls. Here we added the databinding property of the list box control to the `MyTasks` object:

```
<Grid x:Name="ContentPanel2" Grid.Row="1">
  <ListBox x:Name ="lstTasks" ItemsSource="{Binding MyTasks}"
    <ListBox.ItemTemplate>
      <DataTemplate>
        <Grid>
          <Grid.RowDefinitions>
            <RowDefinition />
            <RowDefinition />
            <RowDefinition Height="15" />
          </Grid.RowDefinitions>

          <Grid.ColumnDefinitions>
            <ColumnDefinition Width="150" />
            <ColumnDefinition Width="200" />
            <ColumnDefinition Width="100" />
          </Grid.ColumnDefinitions>

          <TextBlock Grid.Row="0" Grid.Column="0" Text="{Binding
            Name}" FontWeight="Bold" Foreground="OrangeRed"/>
```

```
            <TextBlock Grid.Row="0" Grid.Column="1" Text="{Binding
              DateDue}" />
            <TextBlock Grid.Row="0" Grid.Column="2" Text="{Binding
              Priority}"  Foreground="Yellow"/>
            <TextBlock Grid.Row="1" Grid.ColumnSpan="3"
              Text="{Binding Notes}" />
            <TextBlock Grid.Row="2" Grid.ColumnSpan="3" />
          </Grid>
        </DataTemplate>
      </ListBox.ItemTemplate>
    </ListBox>
  </Grid>
```

15. Press *F5* and you should get the main page displaying the text **View MyTasks List**.

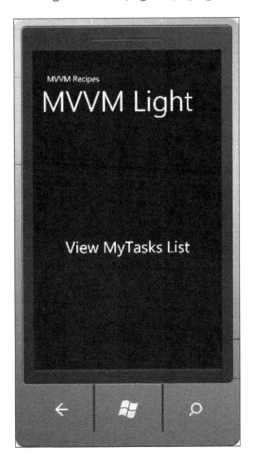

16. Click on **View MyTasks List** to navigate to the MyTasks listing page.

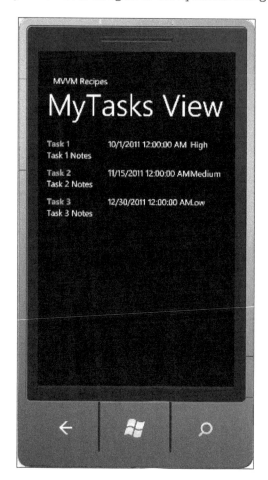

How it works...

The MVVM Light template creates two files in the ViewModel folder, MainViewModel.cs and ViewModelLocator.cs. MainViewModel is the ViewModel class created for each corresponding View file. In this case, it is the MainPage View.

ViewModelLocator class uses the service locator pattern and is used to manage every ViewModel in the project. In the App.xaml.cs file, you will notice that this is used as an application-level resource.

In the `MyTaskView.xaml` file, `Locator` is bound to the page's `DataContext`. You can see this in the last line in the following code:

```
<phone:PhoneApplicationPage
  x:Class="Recipe3_MvvmLightMyTasks.View.MyTaskView"
  xmlns="http://schemas.microsoft.com/winfx/2006/xaml
    /presentation"
  xmlns:x="http://schemas.microsoft.com/winfx/2006/xaml"
  xmlns:phone="clr-namespace:Microsoft.Phone.Controls;
    assembly=Microsoft.Phone"
  xmlns:shell="clr-namespace:Microsoft.Phone.Shell;
    assembly=Microsoft.Phone"
  xmlns:d="http://schemas.microsoft.com/expression/blend/2008"
  xmlns:mc="http://schemas.openxmlformats.org/markup-
compatibility/2006"
  FontFamily="{StaticResource PhoneFontFamilyNormal}"
  FontSize="{StaticResource PhoneFontSizeNormal}"
  Foreground="{StaticResource PhoneForegroundBrush}"
  SupportedOrientations="Portrait"
  Orientation="Portrait"
  mc:Ignorable="d"
  d:DesignWidth="480"
  d:DesignHeight="768"
  shell:SystemTray.IsVisible="True"
  DataContext="{Binding MyTasks,Mode=OneWay,Source={StaticResource
    Locator}}">
```

We then bind the `ListBox` control's `ItemSource` property to the `MyTasks` object.

```
<Grid x:Name="ContentPanel2" Margin="21,17,3,12" Grid.Row="1">
  <ListBox x:Name ="lstTasks" ItemsSource="{Binding MyTasks}"
    Margin="0,6,0,0">
```

In essence, `ModelViewLocator` loads the `ViewModel` and presents the data to the View.

There's more...

In this recipe, we added another simple View to display the tasks list from the static resource. We can use the services we created in *Chapter 7, Windows Communication Framework - WCF*, to get the data and display it in the View. This is the flexibility available in the MVVM pattern.

Also, MVVM Light Toolkit supports Commanding and Messaging features. We can also use the `Command` and `Messaging` classes to eliminate the code behind the event handler for the `TextBlock`'s `MouseLeftButtonDown` event. Here you can use the MVVM Light `Command` to bind the command to the property in the ViewModel. This makes the View completely independent.

See also

Check *Chapter 7* for more on creating the **back-end** data service layer and how to consume it in the Phone 7 client application. For more information on MVVM Light refer to the following two websites:

```
http://www.galasoft.ch/mvvm/#intro
```

```
http://channel9.msdn.com/Shows/SilverlightTV/Silverlight-TV-13-MVVM-
Light-Toolkit
```

Check this article on the Commanding feature of MVVM at:

```
http://www.windowsphonegeek.com/articles/Windows-Phone-Mango-Getting-
Started-with-MVVM-in-10-Minutes
```

Updating the MVVM application

In the preceding recipe, we learned how to use the MVVM Light toolkit to make it easy for us to separate the Views from Models using `ViewModel` classes. In this recipe, we will learn how we can update the view without changing anything in the model side. This recipe demonstrates the MVVM's goal of maintainability by changing the `MyTask View` page.

Getting ready

For this demo, let's use the Phone 7 Toolkit published by Microsoft, which has some nice UI capabilities like `AutoCompleteBox`, `ContextMenu`, `DateTimePickers`, `ListPicker`, `LongListSelector`, `ProgressBar`, and so on. Download the latest version from the following link and install it:

```
http://silverlight.codeplex.com/releases
```

Upon completing the installation, open Visual Studio and select the Toolbox's General Tab. Right-click on and select the `Choose Items` menu. From the Windows Phone Components, select all the items from the `Microsoft.Phone.Controls.Toolkit` assembly and click on **OK**.

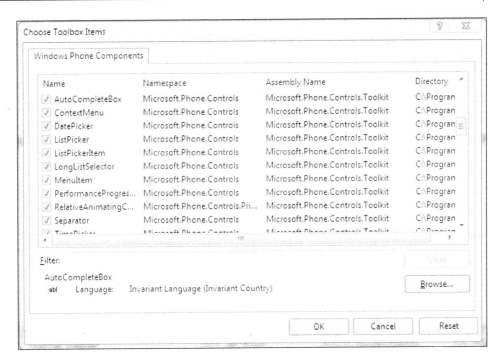

Once you are done, you should see the following controls added to the toolbox:

How to do it...

Let's copy the preceding recipe to another folder, or we can use the same project for this recipe. Let's name the new project `Recipe3_MvvmLightMyTasksUIUpdate`. We will just update the user interface without touching the ViewModel or Model code.

1. Open the `MyTaskView.xaml` file from the `View` folder. Let's add the Phone Resource at the top with a `DataTemplate` each for `Header`, `Footer`, and `ItemTemplate`.

   ```
   <phone:PhoneApplicationPage.Resources>
     <DataTemplate x:Key="TaskListHeader">
       <Border Background="Blue">
         <TextBlock Text="Task Header" />
       </Border>
     </DataTemplate>
     <DataTemplate x:Key="TaskListFooter">
       <Border Background="Blue">
         <TextBlock Text="Task Footer" />
       </Border>
     </DataTemplate>

     <DataTemplate x:Key="TaskItemTemplate">
       <StackPanel Grid.Column="1"  VerticalAlignment="Top">
         <TextBlock Text="{Binding Name}" FontWeight="Bold"
           Foreground="OrangeRed"/>
         <TextBlock Text="{Binding DateDue}" />
         <TextBlock Text="{Binding Priority}" Foreground="Yellow"/>
         <TextBlock Text="{Binding Notes}" />
         <TextBlock Text="-------------------------------------
           ------------------"/>

       </StackPanel>
     </DataTemplate>
   </phone:PhoneApplicationPage.Resources>
   ```

2. Delete the old code for the list box and drag the `LongListSelector` from the toolbox and place it inside the `ContentPanel2` grid:

   ```
   <Grid x:Name="ContentPanel2" Margin="21,17,3,12" Grid.Row="1">
     <toolkit:LongListSelector x:Name="TaskList"
       Background="Transparent" IsFlatList="True"
       ItemsSource="{Binding MyTasks}" ItemTemplate="
         {StaticResource TaskItemTemplate}"
       ListHeaderTemplate="{StaticResource TaskListHeader}"
       ListFooterTemplate="{StaticResource TaskListFooter}" />
   </Grid>
   ```

3. Press *F5* and you should see the new view when you navigate to the **MyTask View** page.

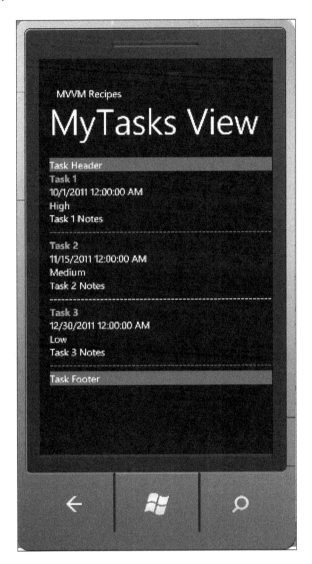

How it works...

In this recipe, we used the more powerful LongListSelector control for displaying the MyTask list view page. We used the header and footer templates of the control to display the blue header and footer. We also set the IsFlatList property to True so it is just a flat list without any fancy features that the control is capable of offering.

Once we are done with the View, we just compile it without touching the ViewModel or Model code. This demonstrates how easy it is to maintain the frontend for any changes and save a lot of development time.

There's more...

You noticed how easy it was to update the View without touching the ViewModel or Model code. Similarly, we can add multiple Views that will use the same ViewModel. We can also update `Model` and `ViewModel` code without affecting the Views. In the next recipe, let's examine how multiple Views with the same `ViewModel` and `Model` work.

Multiple Views with the same ViewModel

Here let's use the preceding recipe and add another View with just a few color changes to the user interface.

1. Open the `MainPage.xaml` file and copy the `TextBlock` control and move it below the first one. Add the new event `MouseLeftButtonDown_1`.

```
<!--ContentPanel - place additional content here-->
<Grid x:Name="ContentGrid" Grid.Row="1">
  <TextBlock Text="{Binding NavName}"
    Style="{StaticResource PhoneTextNormalStyle}"
    HorizontalAlignment="Center"
    VerticalAlignment="Center"
    FontSize="40"
    MouseLeftButtonDown="TextBlock_MouseLeftButtonDown"
    Margin="78,187,86,376" />
  <TextBlock Text="{Binding NavName2}"  Style="{StaticResource
    PhoneTextNormalStyle}"
    HorizontalAlignment="Center"
    VerticalAlignment="Center"
    FontSize="40"
    MouseLeftButtonDown="TextBlock_MouseLeftButtonDown_1"
    Margin="79,291,54,272" />
</Grid>
```

2. Open the `MainPage.xaml.cs` file and add the navigation code as shown in the following code snippet:

```
private void TextBlock_MouseLeftButtonDown_1(object sender,
  System.Windows.Input.MouseButtonEventArgs e)
{
  NavigationService.Navigate(new Uri("/View/MyTaskView2.xaml",
    UriKind.Relative));
}
```

3. Open the `MainViewModel.cs` file and add the property `NavName2`.

```
public string NavName2
{
  get
  {
    return "View MyTasks List 2";
  }
}
```

4. Now copy the `MyTaskView.xaml` file and rename it to `MyTaskView2.xaml`. Open the `MyTaskView2.xaml` file and make a few color changes to the View. Here is the partial listing of the XAML with changes highlighted:

```
<phone:PhoneApplicationPage.Resources>
    <DataTemplate x:Key="TaskListHeader">
      <Border Background="Green">
        <TextBlock Text="Task Header" />
      </Border>
    </DataTemplate>
    <DataTemplate x:Key="TaskListFooter">
      <Border Background="Green">
        <TextBlock Text="Task Footer" />
      </Border>
    </DataTemplate>

    <DataTemplate x:Key="TaskItemTemplate">
      <StackPanel Grid.Column="1"  VerticalAlignment="Top"
        Background="#FFF50F0F">
      <TextBlock Text="{Binding Name}" FontWeight="Bold" />
      <TextBlock Text="{Binding DateDue}" />
      <TextBlock Text="{Binding Priority}"  Foreground="Blue"/>
      <TextBlock Text="{Binding Notes}" />
       <TextBlock Text="-----------------------------------------
          -------------"/>

      </StackPanel>
    </DataTemplate>
</phone:PhoneApplicationPage.Resources>
        ...
        ...
```

5. Press *F5*. You should see two links on the main page. Click on the text **View MyTasks List 2** to navigate to a second View with a different color background. This demonstrates how you can use multiple Views with the same Model data.

See also

For more information on understanding the Phone Toolkit, download the samples and check the different controls provided in the Codeplex site:

`http://silverlight.codeplex.com/releases`

Another MVVM sample from MSDN is found at:

`http://msdn.microsoft.com/en-us/library/gg521153(v=VS.92).aspx`

Check this online resource, which has a complete hands-on lab for creating a sample to-do application using MVVM and SQL CE at:

`http://msdn.microsoft.com/en-gb/WP7MangoTrainingCourse_TodoLocalDatabase`

Also, have a look at this WP7 Dev Guide with many useful links:

`http://www.windowsphonegeek.com/Resources/WP7#wp7`

Index

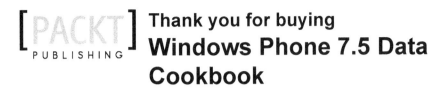

Thank you for buying
Windows Phone 7.5 Data Cookbook

About Packt Publishing

Packt, pronounced 'packed', published its first book "*Mastering phpMyAdmin for Effective MySQL Management*" in April 2004 and subsequently continued to specialize in publishing highly focused books on specific technologies and solutions.

Our books and publications share the experiences of your fellow IT professionals in adapting and customizing today's systems, applications, and frameworks. Our solution based books give you the knowledge and power to customize the software and technologies you're using to get the job done. Packt books are more specific and less general than the IT books you have seen in the past. Our unique business model allows us to bring you more focused information, giving you more of what you need to know, and less of what you don't.

Packt is a modern, yet unique publishing company, which focuses on producing quality, cutting-edge books for communities of developers, administrators, and newbies alike. For more information, please visit our website: www.packtpub.com.

Writing for Packt

We welcome all inquiries from people who are interested in authoring. Book proposals should be sent to author@packtpub.com. If your book idea is still at an early stage and you would like to discuss it first before writing a formal book proposal, contact us; one of our commissioning editors will get in touch with you.

We're not just looking for published authors; if you have strong technical skills but no writing experience, our experienced editors can help you develop a writing career, or simply get some additional reward for your expertise.

Windows Phone 7 Silverlight Cookbook

ISBN: 978-1-84969-116-1   Paperback: 304 pages

All the recipes you need to start creating apps and making money

1. Build sophisticated Windows Phone apps with clean, optimized code.

2. Perform easy to follow recipes to create practical apps.

3. Master the entire workflow from designing your app to publishing it.

Microsoft SharePoint 2010 Enterprise Applications on Windows Phone 7

ISBN: 978-1-84968-258-9   Paperback: 252 pages

Create enterprise-ready websites and applications that access Microsoft SharePoint on Windows Phone 7

1. Provides step-by-step instructions for integrating Windows Phone 7-capable web pages into SharePoint websites.

2. Provides an overview of creating Windows Phone 7 applications that integrate with SharePoint services.

3. Examines Windows Phone 7's enterprise capabilities.

4. Highlights SharePoint communities and their use in a Windows Phone 7-connected enterprise.

Please check **www.PacktPub.com** for information on our titles

Microsoft Windows Azure Development Cookbook

Microsoft Windows Azure Development Cookbook

ISBN: 978-1-84968-222-0   Paperback: 392 pages

Over 80 advanced recipes for developing scalable services with the Windows Azure platform

1. Packed with practical, hands-on cookbook recipes for building advanced, scalable cloud-based services on the Windows Azure platform explained in detail to maximize your learning.

2. Extensive code samples showing how to use advanced features of Windows Azure blobs, tables and queues.

3. Understand remote management of Azure services using the Windows Azure Service Management REST API.

Microsoft Silverlight 4 Business Application Development

Microsoft Silverlight 4 Business Application Development: Beginner's Guide

ISBN: 978-1-847199-76-8   Paperback: 412 pages

Build enterprise-ready business applications with Silverlight

1. An introduction to building enterprise-ready business applications with Silverlight quickly.

2. Get hold of the basic tools and skills needed to get started in Silverlight application development.

3. Integrate different media types, taking the RIA experience further with Silverlight, and much more!

Please check **www.PacktPub.com** for information on our titles

oduct-compliance